rebuilding your message

"Not only preachers and teachers but *every* parish leader and engaged Catholic should read this book. White and Corcoran show us how to communicate so that outsiders feel welcome, insiders grow as disciples, and the Good News of Jesus Christ is unmistakably heard. Here are more great tools for the New Evangelization!"

Most Rev. Thomas Wenski
Archbishop of Miami

"Communication is everything and everything is communication. I wish I had read this book eighteen years ago as I was starting out in parish ministry. Read this book, absorb it, and take control of your message!"

Rev. James Mallon
Author of *Divine Renovation*

"In my fifty years of priesthood, I've met few who match the creativity and insight of Fr. Michael White and Tom Corcoran about parish ministry. Theirs is an exciting path to watch and by which we can all come to recognize that Christ is alive and with us in our midst. He is in our communities—alleluia!"

Msgr. Lloyd Torgerson
Pastor of Saint Monica Catholic Community
Santa Monica, CA

"White and Corcoran are at it again! Thanks be to God! Wisely convinced that what the Church does not need any more of is mediocrity in parish life, they use their creative, innovative style to make the Gospel of Jesus accessible to the people of God. If you're passionate about finding new ways of messaging and thus building the Kingdom of God in your parish, then this is a must-read. These are two wickedly talented guys who the Church needs more of!"

Rev. Tom Hurley
Pastor of Old St. Patrick's Church
Chicago, IL

"'We are the Church' is a conviction that has shaped the religious imagination of so many Catholics today. *Rebuilding Your Message* offers a clear vision and practical strategies for realizing that hope. Focused here on preaching and teaching, White and Corcoran address priests, deacons, staff, volunteers, and parishioners and once again give us a book to inspire, equip, and engage our leaders."

Zeni V. Fox
Professor of Pastoral Theology
Seton Hall University

rebuilding your message

Practical Tools to Strengthen Your Preaching and Teaching

Michael White and Tom Corcoran

Ave Maria Press AVE Notre Dame, Indiana

Founded in 1865, Ave Maria Press is a ministry of the United States Province of Holy
Cross.

www.avemariapress.com

Paperback: ISBN-13 978-1-59471-578-5

E-book: ISBN-13 978-1-59471-579-2

Cover and text design by Andy Wagoner.

Printed and bound in the United States of America.

Library of Congress Cataloging-in-Publication Data
White, Michael, 1958-
  Rebuilding your message : practical tools to strengthen your preaching and teaching /
Michael White and Tom Corcoran.
    pages cm
  Includes bibliographical references.
  ISBN 978-1-59471-578-5 (paperback) -- ISBN 1-59471-578-5 (paperback) -- ISBN
978-1-59471-579-2 (E-book)
  1. Communication--Religious aspects--Christianity. 2. Communication--Religious as-
pects--Catholic Church. 3. Preaching. I. Corcoran, Tom. II. Title.
  BV4319.W45 2015
  251--dc23
                            2015013364

CONTENTS

Part IV: About the Outcomes

PREFACE

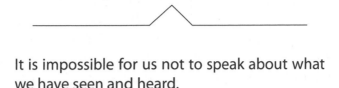

It is impossible for us not to speak about what
we have seen and heard.

—ACTS 4:20

This is not a book about preaching for preachers. This is not a book about
teaching for teachers. This is not a book about marketing for marketers.
This is a book about communication for communicators, who sometimes
preach, often teach, and are constantly in sales. It is about communication
of the most important message ever—the Gospel of Jesus Christ. This is
a book about communication of that life-changing message, which lies at
the heart of our Church, within the local congregation that Catholics call
their parish.

We are two guys who have been involved in nearly every aspect of parish life and leadership. In the process, we have come to understand that all
of it is fundamentally about sharing the Word of God. At the same time,
we've grown aware of how difficult it is to get *any* message across in our
noisy and crowded culture. We have also developed some understanding
about how increasingly indifferent, and at times hostile, that culture is to
what we have to say. Lastly for now, we have learned that when ministers
and leaders get communication wrong in the life of a parish, a lot else goes
wrong, too. When we get it right, church health and growth follow.

We addressed this topic in our book *Rebuilt*, which argues that the
message matters when it comes to the life of a parish community. In *Tools
for Rebuilding*, we offered lots of ideas for communicating, especially when
the form of communication is preaching. We have been heartened by the
positive response those books received, leading us to try our hand at what
follows.

What you will find here are "tools" or strategies for rebuilding the way
you approach your communication. Like *Tools for Rebuilding*, each of the
tools in this book comes in the form of an axiom. An axiom is a starting

point that intends to suggest a basic truth. When employed, that truth, in turn, can determine outcomes. The following axioms were shaped over years in the pulpit and the classroom, during parish meetings and staff workshops. They've been formed before the uninterested and disengaged on Confirmation retreats, the eager and excited at Vacation Bible School, and the relaxed and receptive in adult small groups. Test driven with worshipers during Mass, the grieving at funerals, and the frightened on the first day of class, they have been carefully, painfully, lovingly honed for true believers, the casually committed, sincere skeptics, and the merely bored. These axioms, or tools, have also been informed by the successful strategies of some of the healthiest and fastest-growing churches we've found.

We have organized our axioms into four broad categories suggesting perspectives from which to approach preaching and teaching. They concern your role, your context, your delivery, and the outcomes you can aim for and expect. Gleaned from our own experience, these perspectives provide starting points for you as you begin, or continue, to rebuild your parish's message.

What is herein proposed is offered with humor, humility, and abiding respect for the work you do. And you should know that all our suggestions work, at least in our setting. By employing these strategies in recent years, we have experienced amazing growth in every measurable way: attendance, giving, service, and mission to name a few.

You probably won't agree with everything we have to say. That's okay; take a look anyway. If you're a teacher or preacher, a pastor or church administrator, a key volunteer, or an interested parishioner, you have a role to play in your parish's communication. And that is no minor matter, because the fundamental delivery system for the Gospel of Jesus Christ is the local church community. That's *you*.

INTRODUCTION

THE MESSAGE MATTERS

> In the beginning was the Word, and the Word
> was with God, and the Word was God. He was
> in the beginning with God. . . . And the Word
> became flesh and made his dwelling among us,
> and we saw his glory, the glory as of the Father's
> only Son, full of grace and truth.
>
> —JOHN 1:1–2, 14

Words. They're just words. That's all they are. And sometimes it can feel as if communicating—as a homilist during Mass, a youth minister at a lock-in, a religious educator during a parent's meeting, a business leader to colleagues, or a blogger blogging—is a big waste of time. If you have to make a presentation before your congregation, company, club, or class, it's hard to capture people's attention and harder still to keep it. Sometimes we communicators can feel jealous of chefs and carpenters, and medics and mechanics, who, at the end of the day, have created something they can see and enjoy. After all, we just have words. Like tiny bubbles, perhaps they shine a little in the light before disappearing into thin air, but all too often they seem to have no effect whatsoever.

Yet communication is fundamental to the human experience. It begins at birth. We struggle with it at first and eventually get better, sometimes quite good, but never as good as we want to be and often not as good as we could be.

The message matters, whether it's the infant's cry for food, a teacher's instruction to her students, or the deathbed wishes of a dying man. Even when it seems as if the message doesn't matter, when people are being silly or selfish, or maybe even hateful, they're trying to communicate something, perhaps something profoundly important to them. Scripture says it best: "Death and life are in the power of the tongue" (Prv 18:21).

There is a kind of death that comes from negative or critical words. Recently we were undertaking an expansion of our parking capacity, to accommodate parish growth. We carefully pursued all the requisite approvals and permits with the county and the archdiocese, and we hosted neighborhood meetings. Then, just as the project got underway, one neighbor made a very emotional appeal to as wide an audience as she could reach, including some very influential leaders in the community. She was upset because the view of our property from her family room would be slightly altered. But small as it was, the proposed project led her to communicate in a way that only served to confuse a lot of people, leading to even further miscommunication all around. It felt very unfair to us, and it all happened just because of words.

Words can damage and destroy. They can hurt, and they can kill.

On the other hand, words can bring life and growth. We have been incredibly encouraged by the overwhelmingly positive reviews of our books *Rebuilt* and *Tools for Rebuilding*. Frankly, we were dreading what critics might write, given the strong stance both books take on several controversial topics. While there has certainly been some pushback, the vast majority of comments have been helpful and encouraging.

We have all had experiences wherein words have influenced an outcome, inspired a crowd, or won an election. Each of us has made different choices, set out on new routes, rethought our opinions, or perhaps even reinvented ourselves because of someone's words.

> **Tom:** Many of us have had a favorite teacher who keeps speaking into our lives long after we've left school. I remember one of my sophomore-year teachers describing the human person as a composite of the physical, intellectual, spiritual, social, and emotional. He said that holiness was about continually growing in all of these aspects of our being. Years later, I still return to that definition and consistently use it to evaluate my life.

Father Michael: When it comes to money and giving, both of us have experienced changes of heart (and subsequently giving patterns) because of the preaching of pastors such as Rick Warren who helped us understand what the Bible teaches about money. After hearing God's Word on the subject consistently preached by our evangelical friends, we began tithing and taking seriously the stewardship of our own finances. In turn, that message and those words have rebuilt the financial strength of our ministry as well as how we teach giving in our parish.

There are times when we want to give up but then someone's words compel us to go on. We easily remember a remarkable evening attending a conference in Atlanta. We had traveled there amidst some difficult circumstances back home (*incredibly* difficult). We had almost canceled the trip, planned long before, but went anyway, almost as an escape from our troubles. As the conference started, an announcement was made that the promised keynote speaker would not be speaking, and a substitute would be talking on a completely different topic. We'll never forget the message we heard that night from Dr. Charles Stanley, pastor of First Baptist Church of Atlanta. To our astonishment, he described a situation amazingly like our own and, step by step, he walked us through what he did in that circumstance. He recounted his own struggles, how he persevered and stayed true to his calling. In an instant, we knew what we had to do. It changed our course. It changed our direction. It changed our lives. And that was all because of words.

The message matters. It can change hearts, and it can change worlds. It's Winston Churchill in the dark days of World War II insisting to the people of Britain, "We will never give up!" It's Mahatma Gandhi teaching colonial India, "You must be the change you seek in the world." It's St. John Paul II announcing to Communist Poland, "Be not afraid." Just words—words that changed everything.

This is a book about words, but it is also about more than words. Our words are shaped by the context in which they are presented. The environments we create and the actions we take are also forms of communication. If we fail to pay attention to the setting in which people hear our words, our message will fall on deaf ears. To communicate well—to successfully deliver our messages—our words must work together with body language, environments, and the whole of our lives.

Unfortunately, in our Catholic culture, communication has sometimes been neglected. At least that's our impression. Somewhere along the way, a lot of church people bought the lie that good preaching and teaching are not worth our energy and effort, that no one expects or needs them. As a result, we've all seen lay leaders and ordained alike who never really develop their ability or grow as speakers. We're not criticizing anyone because time and again we've been guilty as charged. Hard to believe, but honestly, for longer than we care to share, we just didn't consider our parish communication all that important.

Yet reason, revelation, and our own experience tell us otherwise. Words have power, and we know from scripture that God's Word has ultimate power. When *spoken*, his Word does not return to him void. That is also true for us: When we use God's Word and do it with skill and conviction and certainly with prayer—in a way that honors and serves the Word—it will not return to us empty or without effect.

The communication that is the fundamental work of our programs and parishes, schools and services can introduce us to God's will, God's plan, and God himself. It can inspire and equip us to conform our lives to Christ. In other words, our preaching and teaching are the primary ways in which the Church reaches the lost and grows disciples.

We respectively present this material in the context of, indeed at the dawn of, what St. John Paul II proclaimed as the "New Evangelization" or the reintroduction of the Gospel into our contemporary culture.

The New Evangelization, by the way, is profoundly countercultural. And you know what? Because it's countercultural, it's a war.

You know what else?

It's a war of words.

Part I
ABOUT YOUR ROLE

1

YOU ARE THE MESSAGE

When I came to you, brothers, proclaiming the mystery of God, I did not come with sublimity of words or of wisdom. For I resolved to know nothing while I was with you except Jesus Christ, and him crucified. I came to you in weakness and fear and much trembling, and my message and my proclamation were not with persuasive [words of] wisdom, but with a demonstration of spirit.

—1 Corinthians 2:1–4

Not so long ago, we witnessed the colossal event of World Youth Day in Brazil, featuring the first foreign trip of Pope Francis. As with everything about this pope's approach, the event turned out to be unexpected and unparalleled. As he began his tour of Rio de Janeiro, thousands of well-wishers, taking advantage of a distinct lack of security, ran beside the small, silver Fiat the pope was riding in, many attempting to shake hands with the pontiff through the open car windows. Officials appeared to lose control of the increasingly chaotic crowd that inadvertently created a massive traffic jam.

Note that this whole encounter happened before World Youth Day actually began. But from the perspective of the worldwide audience that was watching, a powerful message had already been sent. It was a message of God's fondness for us, of his closeness and care. How did the pope manage to do that?

Well, for all his obviously sincere and even delightful expressions of simplicity and humility, the pope understands something many seasoned and sophisticated communicators miss: when it comes to speaking and preaching, *you are the message.* Before you say a single thing, you are already communicating to your audience. And the communication is you. So you should know what *you* are saying.

St. Paul understood that he *himself* was the initial (not the ultimate, not the primary, but the *initial*) message he was communicating. While Paul certainly gave us some of the wisest words ever expressed, he knew words were not where his message started. His message started with a "demonstration of the Spirit," a wordless revealing of some way in which God was working in his life, usually called the fruit of the Spirit. It's the same for us: maybe it's your goodness, your kindness, your gentleness, or your joy. What is it you are telling us about you, and hopefully the Spirit's work in you, before you say a word?

If you're a communicator, what is the message that is *you*?

2

BE YOURSELF

Be eager to present yourself as acceptable to God, a workman who causes no disgrace, imparting the word of truth without deviation.

—2 Timothy 2:15

What is it in human nature, or wherever the tendency lurks, to try to be something we are not? What is it in us that always wants to be cuter, younger, sleeker, faster, smarter, or whatever other things we think we should be better at? And what is it in churchworld that seems to encourage pretense, especially when it comes to pretending that we're perfect people who have all the answers? Being competitive is a fine instinct, and there is nothing wrong with wanting more out of our lives or in our work. But we communicate most effectively when we stay rooted deep down in who we really are—not in who we want to be, not who we want others to see, but us, our genuine selves.

You are the message, but it has to be the *real you*. Easily the most important strategic decision we ever made, when we began to move forward rebuilding our parish, was to just be ourselves and seek the support, guidance, and help we needed. That decision changed everything.

TRY THESE TOOLS

KNOW YOURSELF

It's old but sage advice: Spend quiet time each day and in that time get to know yourself better before God. Take up other effective practices that can assist you, too, such as journaling. Do you really know what is happening to you, what is going on in your life, and what you are feeling and why? Are you in touch with your emotions and in control of your actions and reactions?

LET OTHERS GET TO KNOW YOU

Open the door of your life, your thoughts, and your heart to people whom you trust. Find individuals who know you in your day-to-day activities and others who will be more objective. Give them permission to speak truth into your life so that you gain additional perspective, beyond what you can figure out for yourself. A wise and reliable friend is an excellent place to start. A spiritual director, life coach, or Christian therapist can help you make real progress here. Best advice of all: Get into a small group for faith sharing. If you don't have small groups at your church, start one.

LET YOUR AUDIENCE KNOW YOU

Be comfortable in your own skin. There is nothing quite as attractive as people who know who they are and who are relaxed and at home with themselves. Parishioners will want to listen to you if you can communicate that. (See pages 19–21.)

In two incredible letters that form part of the New Testament, the Apostle Paul shares some unparalleled wisdom with his protégé Timothy. In one place, Paul counsels Timothy to simply be himself before God as a way of more effectively communicating the Word of God. It only makes sense. After all, we are who God has made us to be.

3

HUMBLE YOURSELF

———————————∧—————————————

"Do not fear, Daniel," he continued; "from the
first day you made up your mind to acquire understanding and humble yourself before God,
your prayer was heard."

—DANIEL 10:12

To be yourself, you've probably got to humble yourself to be the most effective communicator you can be. Far from mutually exclusive goals, they
actually go together. In fact, if you're anything like us, one follows pretty
quickly and logically from the other. As we have gotten to know ourselves,
we've learned we have quite a bit to be humble about.

As mentioned, we've spent a number of years serving in a parish. But
really only in the past few years have we come to understand what God is
trying to do through us as we have humbled ourselves (well, at least a little)
before his will.

When we previously refused to do that in our ministry, we experienced
the most frustration, fear, and doubt. We can easily remember season after
season in which we adamantly insisted that we had some great plan or idea
for reviving our parish, only to discover that we were wrong. And then
we had to pretend we weren't and hope nobody noticed. We regularly undertook the amazingly labor-intensive, often embarrassing, usually disap-
pointing, and ultimately futile exercise of acting as if we were experts when,
in fact, we were struggling amateurs.

Undue pride is one of the easiest things to read in a speaker, and usually very quickly it will turn an audience off, or worse, turn it against you.
Humility, on the other hand, is a rare virtue in a communicator. When it
is put together with well-honed communication skills, it has a powerful
impact on an audience and will always win you a hearing.

Father Michael: For reasons that are too complicated and convoluted to share in this context, we decided at one point to try our hand at housing a preschool (it was actually an existing preschool in search of a new location and we wanted to provide that location). Let's just say we thought it was a good next step for us, would make effective use of space that was otherwise not in use Monday through Friday, yield additional income, and potentially bring our parish to the attention of young families in our community. Sounds good, right?

We spent a lot of time explaining all of that to our congregation, and for the most part the news was received with indifference. Flash forward just a couple of years, and we came to realize we had made a mistake. The additional income was inconsequential because the preschool was profoundly intrusive. It regularly interfered with our own daily operations, and it was labor intensive when it came to maintenance. There was absolutely no crossover with school parents and the parish; they were on two different tracks. Worst of all, two of our partners in the project proved themselves to be untrustworthy, and eventually we knew we had to separate ourselves from them. It was and remains a shining illustration of investing in something we had no business being in. We were a church, not a preschool.

We had made a mistake, but in our lack of humility we then made another and tried to unplug the preschool program without any clear explanation to the community. The ensuing outcome was more confusion, misinformation, and hurt feelings than were necessary.

Tom: We approached another experiment in exactly the opposite way. At a certain point, as our weekend Masses became uncomfortably crowded, we decided to try an off-campus video venue. This was to be a Liturgy of the Word, offered in the ballroom of a local hotel, with a video recording of the homily Michael was giving at church. The idea was that even with a full church on parish property, we could continue to welcome unchurched visitors by providing a casual, accessible environment, without any real expense (for construction). It was a great idea, which is effectively working in many churches around the country. We just couldn't make it work in our setting, probably because we didn't try it long enough, and we didn't have any real marketing effort in place for the exercise.

This time we swallowed our pride and acknowledged all that to the congregation. We just humbly admitted that our experiment had not worked and we would be discontinuing it. Frankly, it felt much better than pretending otherwise, and our congregation was quite forgiving.

TRY THESE TOOLS

AS YOU DEVELOP YOUR MESSAGE

Do it with humility. Consider what it is you *are* saying and what it is you *should* be saying. Never miss an opportunity to acknowledge when you're wrong or point out that you've made a mistake.

AS YOU DELIVER YOUR MESSAGE

Adopt a self-effacing approach and self-deprecating humor. At the same time never forget you're standing before God, whom you serve. (See pages 183–184.)

AS YOU EVALUATE YOUR MESSAGE

Was it real? Were you believable? Were you honest and trustworthy? (See pages 19–21.)

Over and over again in the Bible, the wise are counseled to humble themselves. And when they do, God inevitably raises them higher, to greater things. The prophet Daniel is one of the most striking examples of this promise and pattern offered by scripture. In already humbling circumstances, he quite deliberately abased himself even further. And it was this additional humility that turned out to be the path to his influence and success.

Life has a way of humbling us anyway, doesn't it? Why not go ahead, get out in front of it, and do it yourself?

4

CHECK YOUR
EGO AT THE DOOR

John answered and said, "He must increase;
I must decrease."

—JOHN 3:27, 30

A friend of ours, Wayne, runs a successful property management company. One reason he has been so successful is that he understands the sweet spot of his business. Wayne knows exactly the type of buildings and locations that fit his business plan and has learned to stick with properties that will work for it. To maintain this discipline requires wisdom of the heart. When considering a property, he always checks his ego at the door. He noted recently, "If I think that I am interested in a building because I want to see my name on it and that is the main reason I want to buy it, I don't do it." Wayne knows that if his ego is the driving force of his business, eventually he will fail.

However much you naturally or intentionally humble yourself, if you're a communicator, ego can become a problem and you need to guard against that. If you communicate effectively, others will pay attention to you, some will hold you in great affection, and you will be admired and praised. It feels good, flatters your ego, and over time, can become your motivation. On the other hand, we can become overly sensitive, even defensive, in the face of criticism. Our ego can keep us from accepting correction or coaching and then we're not growing as communicators.

When it comes to communication, we have to beware of our ego and work to get it out of the way or better yet check it at the door, because, of course, the point of our communication is not us.

Tom: At times, while preparing for an important message, I have invited other staff members to evaluate a practice run. Frankly, I always feel uncomfortable, even vulnerable, in those exercises; the pride in me wants to put up defenses and push back. It takes an act of will to simply listen to other people's suggestions and recognize that my communication can be better. On the other hand, I must admit to craving positive feedback after I speak. Ego is just a part of communicating.

TRY THESE TOOLS

EXAMINE YOUR MOTIVATION

Ask the Holy Spirit to continually purge your heart and soul of undue pride. When you recognize that ego has slipped in—which will surely happen from time to time, especially when things are going well—acknowledge it and repent of it. Turn back to God.

CONSIDER CRITICISM

Instead of being disappointed or discouraged about criticism, use it as an opportunity to grow in humility. Not all criticism is meant to be helpful; some of it aims to hurt. But before you dismiss critics and criticism, carefully consider if there is truth in it. Beyond that, actively seek out constructive criticism from people you trust and love, criticism from people who have permission to speak into your life, and criticism that supports, encourages, and helps you learn and grow.

(LARGELY) IGNORE ACCOLADES

We think this is usually true. Those who praise you might do so for a lot of reasons, and it almost always feels good, especially initially. But you really can't be putting too much stock in it if you are going to keep your ego in check. Enjoy the praise and then move on.

In the third chapter of John's gospel, John the Baptist's disciples complain that people are leaving him to follow Jesus who is now getting more attention than John. The Baptist responds that it is exactly as it should be, according to God's plan. He even explains that the development is a source of joy for him.

Our communication as parish leaders is all about—and only about—leading people to Christ. We become less so that he will be more.

5

FIRST, LIVE IT

> He rose from supper and took off his outer gar-
> ments. He took a towel and tied it around his
> waist. Then he poured water into a basin and
> began to wash the disciples' feet. . . . He said to
> them, . . . "I have given you a model to follow, so
> that as I have done for you, you should also do."
> —John 13:4–5, 12, 15

Tom: Recently I was in a conversation with some staff members from a number of visiting parishes. One pastor shared his struggle with trying to lead a multicultural community. Others around the table immediately started dispensing advice to the guy, even though, as it turned out, none of them had any experience in such a ministry.

Too often in churchworld, the blind lead the blind. The Greek word *logos* suggests a fundamental concept when it comes to communication. *Logos* means that an audience wants confirmation that we know what we are talking about. When we communicate, our audience is looking for assurance that we have knowledge based on solid experience, not just theory or good ideas. Beyond its inner logic, our message should make sense, not simply because we've studied it, thought a lot about it, and consulted outside experts, but because we have lived it and seen it work.

At the Last Supper, Jesus astonishes his friends one more time. He gets down on his hands and knees and serves them in a wholly humble fashion.

All of it, of course, was only preamble to the service he would perform on the Cross. Calling them into the service of sacrifice, he went first. That is the kind of leader and communicator he wants each of us to be.

The first person whose life should change because of your message is you.

6

MAKE YOUR PERSONAL LIFE PUBLIC

We were determined to share with you not only
the gospel of God, but our very selves as well,
so dearly beloved had you become to us.

—1 THESSALONIANS 2:8

Father Michael: When I go home at the end of the day, my favorite thing to do is sit in my easy chair in front of a roaring fire (it's actually a gas fireplace), devouring the newspaper while watching cable news, not to mention relishing an evening free of meetings. Once in a while, I will watch different kinds of programs, too; I love old movies, especially history and biography. From time to time, I'll even tune in to televangelists. One time I was watching a fellow who, to be honest, was a bit beyond me. Not paying much attention to his sermon, I was more interested in the paper—that is, until he interrupted the fine theological point he was making to tell a story about his personal life. Suddenly, he had my attention. I put the newspaper down and listened to him with complete focus.

Tom: At a staff lunch recently, one team member asked us all to pose for a photo. "Why?" I asked, "What's the occasion?" No occasion, Kristin explained. It's just that every time she posts pictures of our staff on Facebook, it generates increased, sometimes significantly increased, traffic.

Stories and snapshots from behind the scenes naturally draw and, in fact, command our attention. This is especially so when it concerns people with whom we have a relationship. And if you're preaching or teaching, the people you are speaking to have a relationship with you, even if you don't know them. They know *you* and will naturally be interested in knowing more about your story and the details, the behind-the-scenes aspects of your life.

Allowing your personal life to be public makes it easy for your congregation to connect with you; it shows you are a real person, which in turn gives you a stronger platform from which to share spiritual wisdom and guidance. In fact, sharing your personal life builds moral authority.

When preachers or teachers tell stories from their lives, especially ones that include failures or mistakes, they're demonstrating a vulnerability that often yields credibility and trust. This, in turn, encourages others to do the same. When you open up your personal life in a public way, you model how other members of the community can also share their lives with others. You set a tone and establish a culture in which parishioners are sharing their lives with one another.

TRY THESE TOOLS

KNOW THE GROUND RULES

Don't share personal information that is inappropriate or makes your audience uncomfortable. There are things that should simply stay unsaid. Be careful that what you share publically never puts your loved ones down. And when you do share something private, if others are involved, make sure they know beforehand; don't surprise them. Also, it is very legitimate to change names or circumstances to protect the innocent (or the guilty, for that matter).

CONSIDER YOUR PAST

As you work on a message, look for episodes and anecdotes from your past. Think of the stories you find yourself telling to family and friends over and over again. There are key moments in your growth and development, times of discovery or new insights, and funny or unexpected things that just happened to you. You probably have stories worth telling. Use them. (See pages 146–148.)

BE ON THE LOOKOUT FOR CURRENT STORIES

Live with an eye out for experiences you can fashion into useful stories. Mundane things, such as going shopping, and simple stuff like driving your car or time with your family can provide good source material. So look at your present as an opportunity to share. Look particularly close at the different and distinct things you do. We have heard it said, "Interesting speakers have interesting lives." Make sure there are some interesting things going on in your life. Take a class or a trip, go skydiving or mountain climbing, read a book or write one (*that* will make your life really interesting).

St. Paul understood that communication is about building relationships through self-revelation, which is exactly what God did in Christ.

As a servant of the Gospel, you need to be willing to make the same sacrifice. Make your personal life public and your communication will be stronger and more compelling.

7

FORGET SOME OF THE STUFF YOU LEARNED IN SCHOOL

⌃

When Jesus finished these words, the crowds were astonished at his teaching, for he taught them as one having authority, and not as their scribes.

—Matthew 7:28–29

Father Michael: In seminary, I didn't take a single credited course on preaching, teaching, or communications. The only class I did have wasn't even a class; it was an after-school seminar conducted by a priest who was not an effective communicator himself. I sort of learned how to preach in that setting, sort of. Unfortunately, I didn't learn how to preach to the people I would be standing in front of every week. I learned to preach sermons for seminarians; they were my audience, and they evaluated and rated my efforts. So that's who I preached to, giving them what they liked: lots of theology with fine theological nuances, fun facts about the liturgy, great moments in Church history, and insider jokes. All were big values in my seminary sermons. My classmates loved it and gave me positive feedback.

Unfortunately, when I graduated and was ordained, that's how I preached in the parish (pity those poor parishioners). Clever as my homilies could sometimes be, here's what they were not: effective. When it came to evangelization and discipleship, my preaching was more or less worthless.

The challenge for many of us is that we've been deliberately or unintentionally instructed in approaches to preaching and teaching that stand in stark contrast to the very reason we were attracted to it to begin with. We are in Church ministry to reach people far from Christ and to make disciples. To do that, you might actually have to forget what you know or change what you do when it comes to communicating. Acknowledging that is a big step toward fixing the problem.

When Jesus launched the communication campaign that was his public ministry, he astonished his listeners, because he knew how to connect with them, to touch them and change them, and bring them closer to God. And he didn't learn that from the scribes and the Pharisees.

8

DEVELOP YOUR OWN STYLE

Esther put on her royal garments and stood in the inner courtyard, looking toward the royal palace, while the king was seated on his royal throne in the audience chamber, facing the palace doorway. When he saw Queen Esther standing in the courtyard, she won his favor.

—ESTHER 5:1–2

Besides everything else we've talked about when it comes to communication, you've got to develop your own style. Style is all about distinction or distinctive appearance. It refers to substance or quality in presentation.

Tom: I'll admit I have no style.

Father Michael: Seriously, he doesn't.

Tom: In fact, I'll go further and also admit that I am, by disposition, *anti-style*. In high school, as my interest in girls began to awaken, friends started advising me to pay closer attention to my clothes, invest in current fashion, and have my hair styled. I rejected their advice as unnecessary and dismissed their concerns as shallow. I thought of myself as a person of greater depth with little time for such superficialities. Later on, when I started working at the parish, strange as it sounds, this actually affected my communications. I was all about substance and content.

Unfortunately, looking back I can see that the way I was packaging and presenting my message was not serving my message.

Father Michael: I didn't understand that either when I came to work as pastor of a parish. If you had asked me at the time, to the extent that I thought about it at all, I would have said my message was all about the Gospel and had nothing to do with *me*. My goal was to disappear behind the message I was presenting, to get out of the way of God's Word. My strategy was to simply ignore *me*, to pay no attention to how I was coming across. Good goal, bad strategy.

If you really want to ultimately disappear behind the message you are communicating, you've got to do a lot of work on the front end when it comes to *you*. (See pages 6–7.)

As a first-time pastor, I did not realize that in the pulpit I could appear stern; my voice often unwittingly sounded harsh and scolding. I paid little attention to the fact that some of my illustrations did not achieve their desired effect. Worse still, I typically preferred needlessly erudite or overly theological references that made me look smart (or so I thought) but really cast me as out of touch. The overall effect was of an angry, aloof, ungenerous guy who really had no message for the suburban congregation in front of me. Had that assessment been brought to my attention, I would have been horrified.

Some time ago, both of us attended a conference on fundraising and stewardship sponsored by a Catholic diocese. The consultant, who had been engaged to make the keynote presentation, slouched to the podium with a detached, tired kind of posture. He was casually dressed in a way that suggested lack of care rather than comfort. As he plodded through his material, it became obvious he had made the presentation a thousand times before, and we all grew as bored with the information as he had become.

Something else that came across quite clearly: not only the way he looked but also the way he *looked at us* suggested he held his audience in low esteem, as if we were somehow to blame for not knowing what it was he was telling us. He looked condescendingly at us. We're not saying he *was* because we couldn't see into his heart, but he seemed condescending to us and to the parish leaders who were with us. Nothing will turn an audience off faster than a speaker who looks as if he or she doesn't respect them.

It is incredibly important how you look to the people you're trying to communicate with and to know how you look. Your look is a message in itself and can powerfully advance, delay, or even derail what you have to say.

> **Tom:** I will never be stylish, but I have developed and continue to work on my style as a communicator. Basically I like to teach, and in whatever setting I'm speaking, that is how I approach my delivery. Most of the time my teaching is relaxed and casual, but it can also be strong and hard hitting. My humor is dry and understated. When it comes to how I dress for, say, a small-group video, I go for how the typical visitor might show up for church on Sunday.
>
> **Father Michael:** I have learned my own lessons. I realized I needed to lighten up, carefully guard against a stern or grumpy appearance, and use as much humor as possible. My humor is the exact opposite of Tom's (who would have thought) and springs from exaggeration.

The beautiful story of Esther in the Bible is, among other things, an exercise in effective communication. Esther is charged by God with delivering a life-or-death message on behalf of the Israelite people, and time is of the essence. However, the Bible tells us she took time to consider how she looked before she attempted to bring her counsel to the king. Esther won a hearing, in part, based on her peerless beauty, a circumstance the rest of us don't necessarily enjoy. But we can adopt Esther's strategy of investing in what our look is saying about our message.

9

GET IN SHAPE

I drive my body and train it, for fear that, after having preached to others, I myself should be disqualified.

—1 Corinthians 9:27

Tom: I am a big sports fan (that will be a recurring theme). Growing up, I played a lot of basketball, baseball, and football. Sports meant everything to me, and I probably overdid them, but they definitely kept me out of trouble and in shape. As I got older, and the opportunities to play dwindled, I came to recognize that I needed to exercise for my mental, emotional, and physical health. Video workout programs are my current passion, full-body programs with an emphasis on cardio. They're tough and painful at first, but when you discipline yourself and commit to a specific program for an extended period of time, you start to master it and it becomes easier and easier.

In the same way that you have to get in shape to play a team sport or take on a workout program, you have to be in shape when it comes to preaching and teaching. Speaking is difficult, demanding work. It requires stamina and takes a toll. It can wear you out physically and drain you mentally. Author and speaker Michael Hyatt compares a forty-five minute presentation to an eight-hour workday. Really? Yeah, really; try it. So you need to take care of your body and even discipline your thinking if you want to be an effective communicator. It's hard work and requires lots of practice.

Father Michael: No matter who presides, I preach at all the weekend Masses at our church, most weeks of the year from Labor Day to Mother's Day (which is our "high season" of attendance). When I share this practice with other priests, they often express amazement that I can keep up the pace. Typically, they'll respond with comments such as, "I could never handle that much work." When I first took this approach, I could hardly handle it either. I *was* exhausted halfway through the weekend. And it's tiring, but over time my endurance and physical stamina have grown.

Here's how I do it now. For one thing, after the celebration of the sacraments, I keep my message preparation and practice as my number one priority and make no apologies for it. But on the other hand, being completely prepared makes the homily (or message, as we call it) delivery far easier. Being completely prepared is essential to being in "speaking shape." (See pages 59–60.)

Of course there is the question of being physically fit, well rested, and eating right. As we have traveled around the country for our books, we have learned the value of arriving the day before we speak so we can be fresh in our delivery. Your posture is incredibly important to be aware of, too. Good posture will help you develop better stamina.

St. Paul assured the Church at Corinth that he was in shape to share the Gospel with them. Be like Paul, and stay focused on the fact that communication is a full-body workout.

10

YOUR BODY
HAS A LANGUAGE

Samson cried out to the LORD and said, "LORD God, remember me! Strengthen me only this once. . . ." Samson grasped the two middle columns on which the temple rested and braced himself against them, one at his right, the other at his left.

—JUDGES 16:28–29

Probably half of all effective communication is nonverbal. People read our body language and tone before they even hear our words. (See pages 6–7 and 24–26.) Besides your demeanor and your attitude, your body language can powerfully support the message you want to communicate or undermine it. Your body language can bring people to a deeper understanding of your message or completely distract them from it.

TRY THESE TOOLS

STAND FIRM

Tom: Recently, as a part of a school assignment, my son Max had to prepare and deliver a speech to his peers. As I watched him practice, he ceaselessly rocked back and forth. He was unsure of himself, and his nervous energy played itself out as he shifted from one foot to the other. I smiled to myself because that was a problem I also had getting started as a speaker. In fact, it's one I still struggle with from time to time. Shifting from one foot to the other, "dancing," and shuffling all distracts your audience and communicates that you are nervous or perhaps distracted, too. Meanwhile, standing firm communicates confidence, which gives your audience confidence that your message will be worth their time.

USE YOUR HANDS

Father Michael: As a novice preacher, I had this thing going on with my hands (I'm Italian, I can't help it). It was a repeated gesture, bringing my hands together and then flinging them apart, as if I was throwing a ball. People ended up watching my hands instead of listening to me. I never really tackled this problem until I came across and started watching (and then started emulating) a talented preacher who uses his hands in a way that is simply beautiful. In an incredibly artful manner, his hand gestures almost seem to shape and sculpt his words. The way he does it draws his listener into his message. Our hands can subtly, powerfully reinforce what we want to communicate. Open hands can suggest an open heart, an invitation to new behaviors, or a fresh start. Clenched fists might suggest power and passion or underscore a conclusion.

MOVE WELL

Be careful of impulsive movements; sudden, jerky actions or reactions can be distracting and make an audience uncomfortable. Make sure your body moves in rhythm with the message. Stepping forward or leaning into the audience can help emphasize an important point or suggest intimacy. Big, broad gestures can make you look expansive. A sideways stare can communicate humor or satire, and raised eyebrows might mean surprise. The list goes on and on. Think about it; choose deliberately.

The life of Samson is one of the great stories in the Bible. Samson understood his strength and the power of what he did with it. In an eventually dramatic way, he came to understand what effect he could have. Your body has a language; learn to speak with it effectively.

11

IT'S NATURAL
TO BE NERVOUS

Cast all your worries upon him because he cares
for you.

—1 Peter 5:7

Father Michael: Johnny Carson got nervous every day
he taped *The Tonight Show*. Rick Warren still has stage
fright on Sunday mornings. I get at least a little anxious
each time I step into the pulpit, and sometimes, during
Christmas and Easter, for example, I can be trembling
with anxiety. Nerves are often associated with initial or
amateur efforts. But sometimes they can accompany the
work of even the most seasoned professionals.

Nervousness before speaking can be a good sign. It might mean that you
care about what you are doing enough to be concerned you're going to do
it well. Perhaps you're worried that no one is listening or anxious that they
actually *are* and you're going to look foolish or sound stupid. Maybe you're
just afraid of making a mistake.

It's an understandable—sometimes commendable—reaction that must
be overcome. That's because ultimately our nervousness is all about *us*. It
keeps the focus on us. Move beyond that and use your nervous energy to
energize your message. Make sure you breathe properly, keep sufficiently
hydrated, and are relaxed. Imagining (or locating in the assembled crowd)
positive and supportive people will also help. Most of all, remember who
you're working for and what you're trying to accomplish. (See pages 67–68.)

The apostle Peter knew well what it was to be nervous in service to the Lord. More than any of the others, the Bible tells us about Peter's anxiety. He greets the Lord's call with timidity (Lk 5), he sinks in fear when Jesus invites him to walk on water (Mt 14), and he becomes incoherent at the Transfiguration (Mt 17). Most notably, of course, out of pure cowardice he betrays Jesus before the crucifixion (Lk 22).

Later, as leader of the Church, speaking to the faithful as their pastor, he addresses the topic himself. He doesn't deny the reality of nervousness and anxiety even in Christian living and ministry, but he does place it in the proper context of faith and prayer.

12

FIND YOUR BURDEN

Come to me, all you who labor and are bur-
dened, and I will give you rest. Take my yoke
upon you and learn from me, for I am meek and
humble of heart; and you will find rest for yourselves. For my yoke is easy, and my burden light.
—Matthew 11:28–30

To communicate with authority and impact you have to do something that
sounds counterintuitive: you have to find your burden. That is simply all
about discovering the one thing that holds your heart and weighs on your
mind when it comes to your message. Your burden is what you most want
to share with your audience or congregation. Maybe it's just something
that means a great deal to you, given your personal story.

If you don't have a burden, if you can't find one in your material, you've
got the wrong material; at least it's the wrong material for you. When you
do have a burden, you can't wait to preach or teach it. You naturally speak
about it with enthusiasm and excitement, perhaps even passion.

Probably the most intense example of this came in the appeal of our
latest capital campaign. Sometimes such efforts can be far from inspiring
if they focus on needs and costs or bricks and mortar. Our campaign, to
help fund the construction of a new and significantly larger sanctuary, was
decidedly different. We called it "Vision," and it was all about what could
be and should be moving forward as a parish. We based the message on the
conviction God had given us this project, that it was the right project, and
its time had come. In the final Sunday of the appeal, we said this:

"God's vision and God's purposes are inevitable and they will absolutely happen. God's vision is coming. God's vision for this parish is coming.
And this weekend is all about celebrating the commitment that so many

are making to this vision in our community and in our generation. We celebrate and honor your commitment and God will reward it. Vision has an appointed time. Now is the time."

The campaign, by the way, was an unprecedented success but not because of the eloquence of our words or strength of our arguments. It was more about revealing an honest burden from the depths of our hearts.

TRY THESE TOOLS

SPEND TIME WITH SCRIPTURE

What does scripture say that especially excites you? When you spend time with the Word of God, what lifts up your heart and catches your imagination? Why does it excite you? What does it say that resonates with your story? (See pages 50–52 and 149–150.)

PRACTICE THE MESSAGE OUT LOUD

Jesus said that the words we speak are a reflection of our heart. Sometimes your burden emerges from the actual process of practice. The more you practice your message, the more you will discover and come to understand what it is you really want to say. (See pages 59–62.)

CONSIDER THE REAL-LIFE CONSEQUENCES

Imagine that someone you love has come back to church for the first time in a long time. Consider that if they don't find anything compelling or interesting in your message, they may never go to church again and perhaps even give up on God. Speak to that person, and you'll discover your burden. Or find the messages you wish you had known earlier, the direction someone should have given you earlier in life. Indentify the information you could speak to a young version of yourself, or the lessons that you have learned through tough experiences. Your past failures and mistakes are fertile ground for finding the messages that are burdens on your heart. (See pages 19–21.)

One of the most comforting and beautiful of Jesus' teachings comes in Matthew's gospel with his invitation to share our labor and even the burdens of the heart. In exchange he places his burden on us, which is not burdensome at all, because he helps us with it and even carries it for us. As communicators, we should strive to find the heart of our message in what burdens the heart of God.

13

EARN YOUR ETHOS

Moses said to God, "Who am I that I should go to
Pharaoh and bring the Israelites out of Egypt. . . .
Suppose they do not believe me or listen to me?"
—Exodus 3:11, 4:1

Important in any communication, ethos is critical when we are trying to convert people. Ethos is simply the character or attitudes and beliefs that form the culture of a group. The ethos of Catholicism is built around the foundational message that ultimately to find your life, you must lose it; to gain the world, you must lay it aside. We have to convince people that it is in their best interests to sacrifice time, money, energy, control, pride, and much of what they value for life in Christ. The message of the Gospel ultimately challenges people to willingly take up the Cross. If our audience is to ever even consider making such sacrifices, they must believe in us. They will come asking, "Can I trust you or are you just trying to manipulate me? Do you have my best interests in mind or only your own?" You have to build their trust.

TRY THESE TOOLS

BE GENEROUS

Give people permission to *not* do what you want them to do. This is especially important for people who do not have a relationship with Christ or are new to your church. It is absolutely true for the millennial generation and mostly true for everybody else. We naturally distrust a pushy salesperson. But when you tell people they don't have to buy what you're selling, they can take it or leave it, they'll likely have a greater willingness to relax, listen, and learn. As they do, they'll start to trust you. The next time you have something to communicate that is going to be difficult for unchurched people to hear, simply say to them, "You don't have to listen to this." Guess what? They will.

BE VULNERABLE

Share your struggles, tell your horror stories, and reveal your human-ness. Be vulnerable. (See pages 10–13.) This may sound paradoxical, but exposing our failures and weaknesses strengthens the message because truth builds trust. Nobody believes (or particularly likes) the person who pretends to have it all together. We have all been wounded by original sin, and there is something in us that distrusts the person who acts as if they're the exception. Sharing our failures establishes trust with our audience by basing the message in realties they recognize and with which they likely have intimate experience. (See pages 19–21.)

BE LOVING

In *Rebuilt*, we talk a good deal about a mythical figure we named "Timonium Tim." Timonium is where our parish is located, and Tim is the quintessential unchurched person who lives in our community. When approaching teaching and preaching, we always try to do it from Tim's perspective. That means we've got to know the guy, what he's like and what he likes. But beyond that, to be really effective, we've got to learn to love him, too. (See pages 200–201.)

In the amazing dialogue between God and Moses recounted in the book of Exodus, the future leader of the people questions his own credibility with the crowds. Moses is charged with a mighty message, but he fears no one will listen to him and rightly so; not only is he a bad speaker, but also he has zero authority. As the story unfolds, of course, Moses doesn't' ask the people to do anything before he successfully gains their trust and respect.

Don't rely on your position, authority, ordination, or office for credibility. Earn it.

14

IT HURTS TO HEAR YOUR OWN VOICE

For this very reason, make every effort to supplement your faith with virtue, virtue with knowledge, knowledge with self-control, self-control with endurance, endurance with devotion, devotion with mutual affection, mutual affection with love.

—2 Peter 1:5–7

As human beings, we don't know what it is like to be on the other side of *us*. We don't know how we come across to others in our everyday life. We never get to see us, hear us, or talk to us. This is why the scriptures tell us to surround ourselves with wise counselors. We simply need people to help us see our lives from another perspective. Likewise, we probably struggle to evaluate our own communication efforts.

Tom: The best tool for evaluating your skill as a speaker is to watch yourself on video as often as possible or at least listen to audio recordings. Warning: it's painful. I recently suffered through this exercise. I made a presentation and thought it had gone well. Later, watching myself, it became clear that I had overestimated the quality of my effort. My voice was monotone: big expressions, expressions that I thought had been overly dramatic, were actually flat. There were words that were garbled and not easily understood. I even looked somewhat disheveled

and uninterested. The exercise was a humbling but essential reminder of how much room for growth I have as
a speaker.

It hurts to hear your own voice. It is painful to observe how you stand,
your posture, and that angle where the camera is not kind to you. But if
you don't do it, you'll significantly limit your ability to grow as a speaker.
(See pages 6–7, 24–26, and 29–31.)

During a time of terrible persecution for the Church, under the Emperor
Nero, Peter's message in his Second Epistle was one of hope and encouragement for the Christian community. He encouraged the faithful to pursue a
wholehearted integration of the Christian faith into daily living, building
virtue on the foundation of good habits.

The message of our Christian faith, on which all our communication
should be built, is the most important message of all, the most important
message ever. It deserves our best efforts, but these will not be sustained,
much less improved and expanded, without good habits that help us grow.
It hurts, but it helps.

15

IT'S A TEMPLATE

I planted, Apollos watered, but God caused the growth.

—1 Corinthians 3:6

Our parish council meetings are great. The main reason is that, over the years, we have been blessed with great leadership. Our current president is a good example. Ed knows how to run a meeting. So impressive is the organization and energy he brings to the table that you might assume it's because he pours effort and time into preparation—but actually, not so much. As he himself notes, "It's easy. It's a template." Ed chairs our council so effectively because he begins with a basic template, a simple pattern in his head of how meetings work and flow effectively.

Communication and message preparation are difficult. They take work. Wrestling an idea to the ground, determining exactly what we want to say, and then giving shape to how we say it all require effort. (See pages 59–65.) And all the while you're trying to silence the nagging questions: "Will this ever come together? Will this ever make sense?" That said, if you develop a basic process for preparation and presentation, you will find it much easier to survive and even thrive in communication. Rather than hurt your creativity, this discipline actually helps it.

Tom: Take, for example, the preparation for our weekend message (the homily), which follows a well-honed template. It is also a team effort. While only Michael can preach it, several people help to write the message. Our template for preparation is not very complicated. After prayer, we study. (See pages 67–68.) I start with the Sunday readings, relying on some go-to scripture commentaries I

41

always consult. Next, I do a verse-by-verse scripture study, writing out each verse and whatever comes to my mind about that verse. Then, I am finally ready to write. Sometimes, because of the discipline of the process up to this point, I am actually itching to get started, and the writing can often be quite easy. Easy or otherwise, the writing always helps me to further clarify my thoughts. Finally, I deliver Michael a first draft, or as he calls it, a *rough* draft.

Father Michael: Once I have Tom's draft, I focus on the introduction. I ask, "How do I want to begin?" Often I start with a story to acknowledge the commonality of the human experience or introduce some question that creates tension and engages listeners in a journey to find answers. (See pages 169–170.) After that, according to *my* template, I go right for the end: Where do we want to leave people? How do I want to motivate and inspire them? Only then, knowing where the message is coming from and where it's going, do I get down into the deep weeds of the exposition. Meanwhile, our message team is meeting weekly to evaluate my efforts, explore new themes, and plan ahead.

We're not suggesting our way is the only way or the right way for you. But we are encouraging you to develop your own way, create your own template.

The Apostle Paul undertook the groundbreaking work of preaching the Gospel of Jesus Christ to the Gentile world, including the city of Corinth. Paul planted the Church of Corinth before moving on to other missionary activities. Apollos, essentially the pastor of Corinth, worked with the local church, teaching and preaching there, and doing what Paul calls "watering." In time, they recognized that their faith-filled efforts—in the form of a reliable template—were blessed by God, and the church grew.

Your communication efforts will be simpler and far more sustainable if you form a template that works for you and then rely on it, recognizing that at the end of the day it is always God's work, and he makes it effective.

16

MORE GETS CAUGHT THAN TAUGHT

Be imitators of me, as I am of Christ.

—1 Corinthians 11:1

Tom: Kids love to imitate their parents and older siblings. As a father, I have had plenty of opportunity to witness this over and over (and, as the father of seven, over and over and over and over and over) again. That's because, with human nature being what it is, we are wired to learn from others. There's a lot of learning and skill building that come from watching others do what we can't do or what they do better than us. We learn to speak, to walk, and all the other skills we master as children through observation of those ahead of us in life. But that pattern doesn't stop with childhood. When it comes to lifelong learning, more gets caught than taught.

The same is true for our communication skills. If you are a preacher or teacher, you will learn more from watching and listening to great preachers and teachers than any other single thing you do. We have incredible access to such communication; the internet gives us the opportunity to watch and listen to more messages than ever before. Avail yourself of the available resources. (See pages 45–47.)

Watch other preachers and teachers—but don't stop there. Observe sales people sell; watch guides guide. Learn from comedians how to hold the attention of an audience, tell stories, and make use of exaggeration.

Study news anchors and reporters to learn how they use inflection or punch words. Watch great actors and make a habit of carefully studying how they work, how they employ their skill. Even take time to watch, dare we say it, politicians!

The initial and basic instruction St. Paul gives to the Christians of Corinth is just to follow him in his walk with Christ. It was also the most repeated invitation Jesus made to his friends and future disciples: follow me. Infuse your own communication, and preparation for communication, with what you catch in the example of others. Learn and grow from great communicators, and you will be, at the very least, a better one.

17

"CREATIVITY" IS THE ART OF HIDING YOUR SOURCES

———————⌃——————

In times past, God spoke in partial and various ways to our ancestors through the prophets; in these last days, he spoke to us through a son, whom he made heir of all things and through whom he created the universe.

—Hebrews 1:1–2

Father Michael: When I first met Rick Warren, he very graciously commended me on *Rebuilt*. He noted, "I stopped highlighting, because I was highlighting everything. I kept saying to myself, 'I can use this, and I can use that.'" I said, "Thanks Rick, but a lot of that stuff we got from you."

In school, we are taught about the unethical practice of plagiarism. Dishonestly appropriating or simply stealing someone else's thoughts, words, or ideas is a serious offense. Consequently, we are educated in footnotes and endnotes and the various ways to properly cite sources.

While this is important in academic circles and in publishing, in other endeavors it seems, frankly, less so. People borrow from one another all the time and sadly don't always slow down to give credit where perhaps credit is due. From Wall Street to Silicon Valley, everybody is copying everybody else. A friend of ours talks about the importance of R&D—rip off and duplicate—as the key to success in nearly any enterprise. Give credit whenever you possibly can, but borrow and use good ideas for communication, wherever you can and whenever you have the opportunity, if it can help you preach or teach the Gospel.

TRY THESE TOOLS

BORROW IDEAS FROM POPULAR CULTURE

A few years ago, we gave out rubber bracelets impressed with the phrase "Pray 10." We encouraged people to make a habit of praying ten minutes a day, using the bracelet as a reminder. Bracelets, of course, are a commonplace cultural accessory, and our "Pray 10" was a takeoff from the "Play 60" campaign the NFL promotes. Borrowing ideas from popular culture, when done well, can help drive your point home to an audience. Meanwhile, the culture can advertise for you. For example, the next time people saw the Play 60 ad, we think it quite likely that they were reminded of the importance of daily prayer.

BORROW IDEAS FROM OTHER CHURCHES

A church we follow and study advertises on their website, "Use our stuff; we're on the same team." Hopefully, in the Christian world that is true, so why not act like it? We are working together to make disciples for Jesus Christ, and if another church has a great message that can help you do that (and they give you permission), you should go ahead and use it. There have been whole message series, small-group curricula, kids programs, and Vacation Bible School packages we have adapted from other churches. In fact, it's probably fair to say that we learned to develop our own material by first copying others. (See pages 43–44.)

BORROW IDEAS FROM OTHER PREACHERS AND TEACHERS

We borrow phrases or quotes from other speakers we like and use them constantly, especially when someone has a good bottom line or "tweetable" quote. We like to say, for example, "Wise people build their lives around what is eternal and squeeze in what is temporary." We got that from John Ortberg. When we talk about money, we'll always say, "Jesus doesn't want something from you; he wants something for you." We got that from Andy Stanley. "The future starts today, not tomorrow," is something we say regularly that comes from St. John Paul II.

Borrow from others, and when you do, don't just mindlessly mimic what's already been said. You need to make it your own, something that you are comfortable saying that flows from your style. Tweak it to fit your personality and your church, and this will free you somewhat from having to carefully quote and attribute and risk appearing as though you trying to be a carbon copy—which you shouldn't be. (See pages 24–26.)

We learn in the Letter to the Hebrews that the promises and prophecies of the Old Testament are fulfilled in the New Testament. The old covenant is complete in the new covenant who is Jesus. Something similar is true for us. We can stand on the shoulders of others and ethically use their stuff. Use others' ideas, when given permission, to advance the work of the kingdom, *not* to make money. Honestly, ethically, seriously use other people's stuff.

18

BE CREATIVE,
NOT ORIGINAL

But how can they call upon him in whom they
have not believed? And how can they believe
in him of whom they have not heard? And how
can they hear without someone to preach? And
how can people preach unless they are sent?

—Romans 10:14–15

This seems like a painfully obvious statement to make about communication in the Church, but being no strangers to the painfully obvious (our goal is to become the national experts) here goes anyway. We *can be* and *must be* creative, but we really aren't *supposed to be* original.

As communicators in and for the Church, we are charged to serve God's Word in a very disciplined and deliberate way. Being Catholic Christians, we teach the scriptures as given to us by our tradition and taught by the magisterium. That first of all means that we have to *know* what scripture says, and we have to know what the Church teaches. That is a serious responsibility when it comes to our communication.

Embracing this responsibility isn't in the least constricting; on the contrary, it is incredibly liberating and empowering. Think about it: our messages don't come from our own wisdom; they don't need to rely simply on what we know. We don't have to be original, and we never start with a blank page.

On the other hand, our communication of the timeless truth of God's Word must definitely be fresh and should certainly be creative. Given the generation and the culture in which we are working, it should also always reflect the specifics of our time and place.

Paul addresses the basics to the Church in Rome when it comes to Christian communication. Unbelievers come to faith through the message believers proclaim, so someone has got to preach it to them. But preachers and teachers, working in whatever specific settings they find themselves, never work alone or in isolation. We are sent by the Church.

19

TELL THE STORY BEHIND THE STORY

―――――――⌃―――――――

When King Herod heard this, he was greatly troubled, and all Jerusalem with him. Assembling all the chief priests and the scribes of the people, he inquired of them where the Messiah was to be born. They said to him, "In Bethlehem of Judea, for thus it has been written through the prophet . . ."

—MATTHEW 2:3–5

But you, Bethlehem-Ephrathah least among the clans of Judah, from you shall come forth for me one who is to be ruler in Israel.

—MICAH 5:1

One evangelical pastor we know shares an incident from his own small faith-sharing group. At a certain point, they read the story of David and Goliath. After the gathering, one of the members of the group approached him. Our friend explained that this was a well-educated, cradle Catholic who casually confessed that he didn't know that the story of David and Goliath was in the Bible. He thought it was a metaphor derived from a fairy tale. Who, he wondered, was David anyway?

When it comes to scripture, telling the story is important. (See pages 146–148.) Telling the story behind the story is also important. Catholics tend to be spotty, at best, when it comes to scripture. This sad fact is also an opportunity. Telling the story behind the story begins to fill in the gaps and make sense out of what is going on in a given passage. Slow down in your preaching and teaching to peel back the layers of the story: the formation of the Jewish family of faith, the history of the nation of Israel, the life of Jesus, and the birth and growth of the Church. At the same time, establishing the context of the story provides access to the unchurched or unbelieving people in your community. They don't have to feel ignorant or excluded.

Meanwhile, you won't be insulting the intelligence of the biblically literate; you'll be encouraging them in what they do know. Besides, good stories can never be told too often.

Telling the backstory of the passage you're using also increases its impact. We love great lines in movies because of the story behind them. In *Braveheart*, it's easy to remember the line "Every man dies; not every man really lives" because Wallace is about to be executed after a valiant effort. In *Gone with the Wind*, Scarlett O'Hara's starving and impoverished situation leads to her unforgettable vow: "I'll never be hungry again." Or in *The Godfather*, Tom Hagen's rebuff from the vindictive movie mogul leads to the ominous understatement: "Mr. Corleone is a man who insists on hearing bad news at once."

TRY THESE TOOLS

KNOW THE STORY YOURSELF

Before you present, reread the story and make sure *you* understand how the passage you are presenting fits into the larger story of salvation history. If you don't know it, learn it. If you've forgotten, relearn. You need to have a feel for what was going on. Put yourself in the story, and imagine what it felt like to be a part of it.

KNOW THE PART OF THE STORY YOU WANT TO SHARE

Some details add flavor to the story, while others create distractions. When presenting the story, discern what needs to stay in and what is merely distracting or confusing.

KNOW YOUR EVENTUAL BOTTOM LINE

Where is this story going? How does it end? Where does it land? Make sure you know that as you begin, you allow the ending to shape the beginning and the middle part, too.

The beautiful narrative of the Nativity centers on the unexpected locale of Bethlehem. Why? It was the birthplace of Israel's greatest king, David, and would also see the birth of Israel's eternal king, Jesus Christ. Matthew knew the story behind the story in scripture and connects the dots for us. That was a powerful thing to do because suddenly the story got bigger.

20

FOCUS FOR GREATER IMPACT

⌃

I have much more to tell you, but you cannot bear it now.

—JOHN 16:12

Both the sun and a laser beam emit light, but the sun is obviously immense and a laser only the size of a pinhole. Yet the laser can cut through steel; the sun, from our experience, cannot. How does that work? Intensity of focus.

A huge key to effectiveness in any enterprise or endeavor is focus. It allows us to make a greater impact and, over time, build momentum. And it is often more powerful than a shotgun approach, nowhere more so than in communication.

Effective communication requires focus. And in our parishes, it could make all the difference; it could make more difference than anything else, in terms of effective evangelization and discipleship.

TRY THESE TOOLS

DECIDE ON A CENTRAL POINT

Your message has (or needs) a point or a central conceit. Place it squarely at the heart of your message, and return to it over and over again. Keep your focus on it in order to attract and maintain your audience's focus.

FOCUS ON A SINGLE PASSAGE

In any given message, focus on one scripture passage or even a single verse and milk it for all that its worth (and given that we are dealing with the Word of God, its worth is limitless). Slow down over a phrase, step into a scene, and describe it in detail; help your audience see it.

OFFER A SINGLE CHALLENGE

And when it comes to any challenge you level at your audience, make it a single challenge, not a laundry list. Let your listeners decide whether or not they are going to take the specific step you are describing, but don't give them a free pass with a menu of options.

Jesus prepares his friends and followers for the coming events of the Passion by helping them focus their attention on what they need to know, what will get them through it all. You will grow in your role as a communicator as you learn how to focus.

21

LET YOUR MESSAGE MARINATE

The child remained in the service of the LORD
under the priest Eli.

—1 SAMUEL 2:11

And Jesus advanced [in] wisdom and age and
favor before God and man.

—LUKE 2:52

Tom: I like to grill, and I grill old school. There's none of
that gas grilling for me—it's all about that charcoal flame.
I am a dedicated student of *Weber's Art of the Grill*, the
authoritative and classic guide for serious grillers everywhere. Over the years, I have worked through many of the
recipes. Along the way, I have discovered the power of
marinating (the process of soaking the meat in seasoned
liquid before grilling). It can tenderize all types of meat,
and it's the easiest way to infuse flavor into your food and
add excitement to a meal. But it's only effective if you think
ahead. Last minute marinades really don't work; they can't
achieve the full flavor. To do that, you need to start a marinade in the morning of your cooking and, for tougher
cuts of meat, such as London broil, the night before.

If your habit is to pull a message together the evening before the morning
you're scheduled to deliver it, and if you only write on the edge of a deadline,

you might be depriving yourself and your audience of the impact you could be having. There are probably people who work best like that but not many.

A good message needs to marinate because the marinade provides the flavor. It can soften up what might otherwise be difficult or challenging to digest. It can be the point in the process where humor or interesting illustrations emerge.

TRY THESE TOOLS

PLAN LONG TERM

You should plan all your communication as far in advance as possible. If you're preaching, plan out a season or even an entire liturgical year. If you're teaching or responsible for adult faith formation, look ahead each semester to the next semester.

USE YOUR PLAN AS A LENS

Your plan can be a vantage point or lens through which you read books, interpret experiences, and watch movies. You can be on the lookout for what you can "use." You can be reflecting on it in the shower, when driving to work, or while cutting the lawn.

START IMMEDIATE PREP EARLY

Don't sit down to write your Sunday-morning homily on Saturday night; don't wait till you're on your way to your presentation to pull your notes together. Do it as many days ahead as you can, even if it just sits on your desk. Sit with it.

As with the great prophet Samuel, Jesus spent his youth in total obscurity, unknown and seemingly without purpose or direction. But in fact, God's plan was unfolding in the lives of each of these men, and they had the wisdom to wait for him to complete the process.

22

EQUIP YOUR SETTING AND YOURSELF

Go into the city and a man will meet you, carrying a jar of water. Follow him. Wherever he enters, say to the master of the house, "The Teacher says, 'Where is my guest room where I may eat the Passover with my disciples?'" Then he will show you a large upper room furnished and ready. Make the preparations for us there.

—Mark 14:13–15

We wrote this chapter and then considered deleting it. It all seems so obvious.

In any craft or skilled effort, there is a need to prepare your setting before getting to work. A painter clears away furniture, covers outlets, cleans, and primes surfaces; a surgeon arranges surgical instruments and lighting and carefully scrubs; pilots check and recheck the instrument panels and arrange themselves in the cockpit. As skilled workers prepare physical settings for their work, they mentally prepare.

The same is true for communication. We need to prepare the setting *and* ourselves.

TRY THESE TOOLS

PREPARE YOUR SOUND

Check out the sound system you are using, *every time* you use it, no matter how often you use it. Obviously this is especially important if

you are in a setting not your own. Spare your audience the unpleas-
antness of a sound-check adjustment as the introduction to your
presentation.

PREPARE YOUR PLACE

Get to know exactly where you are speaking: a stage, a podium, or
a table? Arrange your notes in a way that is easy for you to access.
Check that the lighting works for you and you can clearly see your
notes. (See pages 144–145.) Make sure you have water.

PREPARE YOURSELF

It is important when we are speaking not to show up at the last minute. Instead, provide yourself plenty of time, with lots of margin both
before and after you speak. Also, put together a little routine before
you start speaking. No kidding, this can really make a difference.

> **Tom:** Mine goes like this: I practice a breathing exercise
> in which I breathe in deeply and modulate my breath.
> And I have a little prayer I pray, quoting Psalm 51. I pray,
> "Lord open my lips and my mouth shall proclaim your
> praise." This helps me to relax and calls on God to speak
> through me.

> **Father Michael:** Before speaking I can often feel anxious
> or stressed, and I find that music can calm me down and
> even out my emotions.

The whole cycle of the Lord's passion, death, and resurrection is set in
motion by some simple steps of preparation. And yet they are considered
important enough to be included in Mark's remarkably concise account of
Jesus' life. Take the lead from the Lord, and prepare your setting, making
sure you have everything you need.

23

PREPARATION SHINES THROUGH

A voice proclaims: In the wilderness prepare the way of the Lord! Make straight in the wasteland a highway for our God!

—Isaiah 40:3

Preparation is the action or process of making ready, of equipping for use or consideration. If your message is to be useful and worth considering for your audience, it will require preparation.

Easily, sometimes instantly, preparation shines through. And lack of preparation is even easier to recognize. We have all listened to presentations when it was clear that the presenter was just winging it. That can be a very painful experience for an audience and, for an inexperienced speaker, a paralyzing ordeal. Even for those who are talented enough to get by regularly without preparation, there is that nagging feeling that the message could have been better.

At the end of the day, there is no substitute for preparation. It builds confidence in speaker and audience alike and helps everybody relax. Preparation insures energy, too. And the more you prepare, the more conversational your message will sound and flow out of who you really are. (See pages 134–135.)

Most of us intuitively know that we've got to prepare. The problem is that everything and anything will conspire to distract us from the task. We have to learn to jealously guard the time we need.

How much time do you need? That depends on the type of presentation, as well as your familiarity with the material. When it comes to new material, we've heard different answers to the question. Pastor Rick Warren of Saddleback Church puts sixteen hours into his sermon preparation every week he preaches. Pastor Perry Noble of New Spring Church advises putting in an *hour* for every *minute* you talk.

> **Father Michael:** I set aside at least ten hours per week to work on my weekend homily. I work from a draft Tom has prepared for me that he's probably put five to six total hours into. (See pages 41–42). We didn't start with that kind of commitment to preparation. We had to work up to it. Set a goal for how much time you would like to work on your message. Then, honestly evaluate how much time you actually take to prepare it, and start looking for ways to bridge the gap.

The prophet Isaiah forecasts the advent of John the Baptist's preaching ministry. In fact, all of the Old Testament prophets are preparatory for John, the final and greatest prophet, because he points directly to the coming of the Christ. If God took a thousand years to prepare for his greatest sermon, Jesus of Nazareth, doesn't our communication deserve all the time we can give it?

24

SPEAK LIFE INTO THE MESSAGE

Then he said to me: Prophesy over these bones, and say to them: Dry bones, hear the word of the LORD! Thus says the LORD GOD to these bones: Listen! I will make breath enter you so you may come to life. . . . Then you shall know that I am the LORD.

—EZEKIEL 37:4–6

Tom: I have a bucket list goal to do a stand-up comedy routine one day, and this is a tough goal for me since I'm not funny. One year for my birthday, my wife, Mia, gave me a book of interviews with famous stand-up comedians. Each comic discussed comedy as well as the process they have for producing their material. Almost all of them acknowledged that they begin their preparation by writing. Some in fact described themselves as writers first and foremost.

But it is also clear their success hinges on the ability to move from the written word to the spoken word, that they use to engage their audiences. They know they eventually have to give voice to their presentation.

Some of our communication, such as blogging or tweeting, is exclusively written communication. That's the point and that's the destination. Written text is not the point or the destination for teaching and preaching. And we contend that writing, difficult as it is for all of us, is actually *easier* than speaking. Of course, most people can simply talk off the top of their heads. But making an *effective* oral presentation is one of the most challenging ways to communicate. That's because your presentation is an elaboration and amplification of your written work. Writing is only part of the journey. At some point, sooner or later, the speaker must step away from the written word and speak life into the message.

That means you need to practice it out loud. That sounds obvious but is often overlooked entirely in preparation. Speaking it out loud begins to give rhythm and flow to your message that a written piece won't necessarily have, however well written it is. It is here that you will begin to form transitions that your written work won't always need. Speaking it into life helps you learn when to take a breath and where to pause in your presentation.

Speaking it into life uncovers your passion and heart for the message. It also helps you to find the inner logic of your presentation in a deeper way. Sometimes, often actually, in rehearsing a message we've found ourselves acknowledging, "Oh, *that's* what I want to say!" (See pages 34–36.)

In his vision of the valley of dry bones, Ezekiel receives a message of hope for Israel. He *receives* the message, but nothing happens until he *speaks* the message. He speaks the message into life, literally. And with it the bones themselves come to life, symbolizing Israel's resurrection and renewal. You need to speak life into your message.

25

PRACTICE MORE THAN YOU PLAY

Then David told Saul: "Your servant used to tend his father's sheep, and whenever a lion or a bear came to carry off a sheep from the flock, I would chase after it. . . . The same LORD who delivered me from the claws of the lion and the bear will deliver me from the hand of this Philistine."

—1 SAMUEL 17:34–35, 37

Until I arrive, attend to the reading, exhortation, and teaching. Do not neglect the gift you have, which was conferred on you through the prophetic word with the imposition of hands of the presbyterate. Be diligent in these matters, be absorbed in them, so that your progress may be evident to everyone.

—1 TIMOTHY 4:13–15

Tom: When you watch professional sports, the athletes make it look easy. Baseball players seem to swing effortlessly. NFL quarterbacks throw the ball with the same ease you might toss it around your backyard. It isn't easy. It only looks that way.

Any time you see someone make something exceptional appear easy, something significant seem simple,

whether it is athletics, acting, cooking, or crafts, anything
really, you can be sure they have put many, many more
hours in preparing to do it than in actually doing it. It
looks easy because it has become natural to them as they
have developed their abilities.

Communication is the same way: it's a craft and that takes practice. (See
page 153.) Not just preparation, it is so much more than preparation; it's
about doing it over and over again. To become an effective communicator,
you have to work on developing your talent. Perhaps one of the weaknesses
in our Catholic culture is not a lack of talent but a lack of *developed* talent.
Many intentionally growing churches (i.e., evangelical churches) enjoy the
reputation of great preaching and teaching not because they have more talent but because they have placed more emphasis on developing the talent
they have.

   We need to learn from the great speakers and communicators of our
generation, people such as St. John Paul II, Pastor Andy Stanley, and author Patrick Lencioni. When you hear Patrick speak, his humor and wisdom seem off the cuff; Andy sounds casual and conversational; and St.
John Paul II obviously spoke from his heart. But what looks easy and effortless is the product of talent carefully honed over disciplined work time
and eventually a lifetime, a lifestyle based in the willingness to practice.

   In his book *Outliers*, Malcolm Gladwell studied different disciplines
and their respective experts, everyone from Bill Gates to the Beatles. Gladwell found that, on average, it took even the most amazingly talented people about ten thousand hours of practice to become an expert in any field.

TRY THESE TOOLS

FIND TIME

Carve out time in your schedule when you can practice. Maybe you
don't have an extra ten thousand hours to spare, but you probably
have extra time somewhere. It is important to find not only time but
also the right time when you are at your best.

FIND SPACE

Find a place away from other people and your telephone and *all* your electronics. Practice free from distractions to the fullest extent possible.

FIND THE DISCIPLINE

Get things off your schedule that keep you from practicing. In our experience, this is a constant challenge and a daily discipline, even more challenging than finding time for writing or preparation. The world, the flesh, and the devil will always and everywhere conspire to rob you of the discipline you need to be the most effective communicator you can be. In most parishes there is always more to do, and so many things are presented as urgent. Sadly, the first things to be sacrificed will often be preparation and practice. Make a schedule and discipline yourself, and those around you, to safeguard it. You might just have to stop doing some things you're doing right now. If so, you might find others better suited to those tasks.

As a communicator, you may well feel as if you never have enough time to devote to your craft. Maybe that just goes with the craft; maybe it just goes with any disciplined effort. If you feel that way, it could mean God has given you a deep *desire* to communicate and you're in the right line of work.

Nobody is born great. Case in point: David. He spent years in obscurity tending sheep. Maybe he felt as if he was wasting his time, but he was actually building his strength and skill before he ever faced the giant, Goliath.

Nobody is born without talent. Case in point: Timothy. And that's why Paul lists his gifts and encourages him not to neglect them despite the tendency in human nature to do just that.

Great talent is a gift *and* a choice. Start working on the talent you've been given, and get good at it. Then get great.

Part II
ABOUT YOUR CONTEXT

26

BEGIN IN PRAYER

⌃

Jonah prayed to the LORD, his God, from the belly of the fish. . . . The word of the LORD came to Jonah a second time: Set out for the great city of Nineveh, and announce to it the message that I will tell you.

—JONAH 2:2, 3:1–2

Father Michael: At my ordination as a deacon, I was given the duty and the privilege of preaching, which I enjoyed from the first. However, as I approached this responsibility, week after week, year after year, when Monday rolled back around I didn't even know where to start. I faced a blank slate, always unsure of how to begin filling it. Sometimes I started with exegesis, or textual analysis (such as it was, given my limited background in scripture). Other times, I began by searching for an attention getter. If it was good enough or funny enough, it didn't really matter what followed, right? Over the years, I more and more relied on the bad habit of simply reaching back into my files to see what I had said before on a given reading or Sunday and just freshened it up, hoping nobody noticed (they always did, by the way).

Tom: I could say the same about being a brand-new youth minister speaking to teens. I wasted a huge amount of time just trying to get started.

The point is, when it came to communicating, we had no idea where to begin. And since we were in a parish, with the mission of sharing God's Word, *that* was a somewhat curious situation to be in. We were missing a rather obvious point. As Christ followers, the very best way to start anything, from a meeting to a meal, is in prayer.

TRY THESE TOOLS

PAUSE PRAYERFULLY

Before jumping into message preparation, stop, pause, and find the time and a good place for prayer. Pray that God guides the process and gives you the message he has in mind. Let it be his message, the one he wants, not merely yours.

STUDY PRAYERFULLY

Next, whatever style of message you are preparing, use scripture and approach it with the view of finding the message God is asking you to communicate. Even if your message isn't a liturgical homily, it can be based in God's Word and find life from it. Spend time with the text, not in an academic way, but in a prayerful, humble way. (See pages 10–13 and 34–36.)

PREPARE PRAYERFULLY

Proceed in prayer, write prayerfully, and practice your message prayerfully, as a form of prayer.

In the Bible, the prophet Jonah is, to say the least, a reluctant prophet. He does everything he can to resist the mission God is giving him. In the process, he gets himself into a lot of trouble. The way forward comes when he (finally) turns to God in prayer. There he discovers the message God is asking him to deliver and precisely how to deliver it. He still has plenty of work ahead of him, but in prayer he is well on his way to becoming the communicator God has shaped him to be.

27

YOUR CAMPUS *IS* SAYING SOMETHING

> As he was making his way out of the temple area one of his disciples said to him, "Look, teacher, what stones and what buildings!"
> —Mark 13:1

When we first came to Nativity, we heard one comment from outsiders over and over again. It initially surprised us, subsequently annoyed us, and eventually motivated us to action. People would say, "I never knew there was a church back there." "Back there" refers to the woods that more or less surround our campus. But don't think we are in an obscure location; we sit near a major intersection of one of the busiest roads in the State of Maryland. Walgreens recently paid ten million dollars for a small lot adjacent to our property. That's how desirable is our location. But most people, including most people in our immediate neighborhood, did not know we were here. How did that happen?

There are lots of reasons, but probably one of the main ones was our entrance.

It was densely overgrown, the driveway itself poorly maintained, and typically chained off with a rusted old chain. The church's sign was actually an eyesore, hard to read, and easy to miss, with faded, peeling paint. True, this entrance was largely ignored by passersby, but it was definitely communicating a subtly sad message. The neglect was effectively telling people there was nothing here for them, nothing of any interest or value. More or less it was saying "we're closed."

Communication in your community begins with your campus, and your campus communication begins with the entrance. So take a look at it. Determine if it attracts people or turns them away. If you are on a major road, your signage presents a great opportunity for outreach and making a positive first impression. Regardless of your location, you should make sure your sign reflects who you are.

After that, complete a careful assessment of the general state of your whole campus, all of which is telling people about you and your church's message long before you ever get a chance to. Drive down your driveway, walk up the front steps, and around the perimeter of your building. Take a good look. Ask yourself, if you knew nothing else about the parish beyond this view, what would it be telling you? Uncut grass, dead shrubs, dirty sidewalks, clutter, and trash all communicate you don't care about your campus. That in turn communicates to your guests—if only at a subconscious level—that you don't care about them. Maybe that doesn't seem fair, but it's true.

The vast magnificence of the temple in Jerusalem, as adorned by King Herod the Great, has only recently been discovered through archeological investigation. It was meant to make a big statement to visitors and, as the gospels tells us, it certainly did for the apostles.

When it comes to the unchurched, massive and magnificent matter not in the least; clean and cared for are much more important. We've visited some of the biggest, most successful churches in the world, and we've been to some entirely modest communities, too. And sometimes we've actually had the same reaction in both. In visiting successful, healthy churches, of whatever size, we've almost always found ourselves thinking, if not saying, "Somebody cares about how this place looks." And this always makes us think, that's the kind of church we want to be, too.

28

DON'T SELL ANYTHING IN YOUR LOBBY

Then Jesus entered the temple area and proceeded to drive out those who were selling things, saying to them, "It is written, 'My house shall be a house of prayer, but you have made it a den of thieves.'"

—Luke 19:45–46

You may or may not have a spacious lobby, and if you don't, there is probably not much you can do about that. But your building has some specific point or points of entry for your guests and first-time visitors, and it is communicating something. You can shape that communication.

The best lobby areas we've seen are clean, of course; that is a given. If it's not clean, you're not even in the game. We all clean our homes when guests are coming. You wouldn't think of doing otherwise. Cleanliness says, "We're waiting for you; we're ready for you." The same applies for your church lobby. It needs to be clean.

But cleanliness isn't enough. Your lobby must evidence a distinct lack of clutter because clutter is probably more about church people than guests. This includes an absence of furniture that is not explicitly for the convenience of guests. Clutter also comes in the form of advertisements and bulletin boards, often carrying outdated or irrelevant information. Many churches go to great lengths to try to attract people's attention in their entry experience. If your lobby is saying anything more than "Hello, welcome, we're glad you're here," it's saying too much. Don't say too much. (See pages 132–133.)

If you have the space and the technology, it is also great to equip your lobby with sight and sound from the sanctuary. This is a simple and subtle way to begin to introduce latecomers to the worship experience, assist people with special needs, and provide a real service to parents with toddlers. (See pages 73–76.)

Here's the main thing: don't sell anything in your lobby. We mean it. Don't sell anything. Jesus doesn't like it.

29

GO FOR THE LOW-HANGING FRUIT

Then children were brought to him that he might lay his hands on them and pray. . . . Jesus said, "Let the children come to me, and do not prevent them; for the kingdom of heaven belongs to such as these."

—Matthew 19:13–14

Parents with kids need lots of help, and the younger the kids, the more help they need. Interestingly, in our community many parents, perhaps most, still want some kind of religion or religious experience for their children. It certainly comes as a priority only *after* sports and school, but it is still there on the list. Even among unchurched parents, it's still there. We don't know exactly why that is. Perhaps they implicitly understand the need to root their children in a solid tradition or yoke their parenting to a higher authority. Anyway, when it comes to churchworld, parents are definitely looking for help and absolutely appreciate it.

If we can reach parents with young children, we score a double win. Getting kids excited about coming to church is forming a firm foundation of faith for them and reintroducing their parents to the Mass. When it comes to evangelization, this is definitely an available, even easy, win.

We believe it most effectively happens in space specifically dedicated to kids' weekend worship apart from the main sanctuary. We know not everyone agrees with us, especially a lot of moms who bravely bring their young children to Mass and struggle to keep them there. They do so each week despite the near impossibility of not disrupting the liturgy and distracting worshipers and liturgical ministers alike. They and their children often end up miserable. We think there is a better way for everyone, and it starts in designated areas apart from Mass, not as an *exclusion* of our young members but as an *accommodation* of them; not a *substitution* for Mass but a *preparation* for it. We like to say our children's environments are created so that they have great spaces in which to "play, worship, learn." In a pattern that mirrors the shape of the liturgy, kids gather for fun, which transitions into worship and bible storytelling. If children are introduced to our church through these environments, they will learn the liturgy and how to act in it, and they will learn to love it.

However, if our children's environments don't communicate the right message, parents will not be comfortable leaving kids with us, and rather than taking ground for God's kingdom we lose it.

TRY THESE TOOLS

SAFETY

Your kids' area first must communicate safety. In our society that constantly warns of dangers and threats coming at our children in myriad ways, this is a parents' primary concern. Of course, foundational to all children's programs are child-protection requirements now in place in each diocese and presumably in each Catholic parish. But such procedures and requirements are, by their very nature, behind-the-scenes exercises. Our programs must not only be safe; they must *communicate* safety. Communicating safety is not as important as the *actual* safety of children, but it is critically important if parents will actually ever use your kids' programs.

You communicate safety by having a team or multiple teams of volunteers (depending on the size of your program) who are providing layers of security and service. One adult (who is a stranger to your guest) does not communicate that their kids will be safe. A *team* does. In our children's ministry, we have not only volunteers who work with the kids but also additional ministers we call hosts. Their job is actually to work with parents, greeting them and answering their questions.

Another way to communicate safety is through some established and consistent check-in. Regardless of style, a check-in-and-out system tells parents that their child is, and stays, where they're supposed to be. Our own process has evolved over the years along with the available technology. Currently everything runs through our parish database and connects with parents' smartphones. When checking in, parents simply type in their numbers, their children's names pop up on the screen, and a nametag (complete with any allergies) is printed. If a family is new, they can register there, too.

CLEANLINESS

Do we even have to say it?

After safety, we want our children's space to communicate conditions promoting health and hygiene.

> **Tom:** Recently, I attended another parish, elsewhere in our region, for a holy day Mass. I went with my family, and given our large number of small kids, we sat in the "cry room." The room looked as if it hadn't been cleaned in years. There was actually trash littering the floor, and the carpets were old and stained. The chairs were dirty and the walls very much in need of a fresh coat of paint. Even the window, providing a view of the sanctuary, was so smudged it was difficult to see through. Handwritten signs, posted randomly on the walls, looked old and outdated. The whole place just felt filthy, and all I wanted to do was leave.

Cleanliness and safety go hand in hand. If the look of a place doesn't communicate that it is regularly cleaned and cared for, if it is disheveled or even dirty, we also assume that the space is not safe.

Here's a funny fact: children's space communicates cleanliness most easily when we actually go ahead and *clean it*. In between every Mass, our volunteer ministers take a few minutes to wipe down the surfaces and toys with disinfecting wipes and generally freshen things up. Every Monday, our children's spaces are thoroughly cleaned from top to bottom. A few times a year, we also do a "deep clean," essentially taking everything out, cleaning the space, cleaning everything that was in the space, and then putting it all back together again. This can all be done by volunteers.

Another way to communicate cleanliness in our children's areas is to have only a few toys. Many nurseries and children's areas we've seen are overrun with junk (usually old stuff that's been "donated" by people who want to get rid of it but don't want to throw it away). Cluttered spaces communicate, well, clutter. Nobody wants their kids in your clutter.

FUN

Along with cleanliness and safety, we want our children's areas to communicate welcome and hospitality. When new people check out our programs, we want them to know that we are glad that they and their children have joined us. For kids themselves, the most effective way to communicate hospitality is to make the place *look* fun. We want our children's programs to look fun. Vibrant colors, friendly volunteer ministers, and wide-open accessible spaces all suggest that church is a good place to be for kids. But decorations also need to be at adult eye level so parents appreciate that, too.

Matthew, Mark, and Luke all tell us of Jesus' rebuke to his own disciples when it came to children's ministry. Jesus insisted that the kind of community he was establishing would be a safe and inviting place for them to be. It is the same for our parishes. And when they are, we are communicating a powerful message to parents and grandparents, in fact, all adults. It's an easy win and a great opportunity. You could call it the "low-hanging fruit." Go for it.

30

IT NEEDS TO BE WORTHY OF MYSTERY

They are to make a sanctuary for me, that I may dwell in their midst.

—Exodus 25:8

The celebration of the Eucharist requires only a few simple things: first, the primary elements of bread and wine. Then there are the altar, the ambo to enthrone God's Word, and a place for the assembly. Add to these the chair of the priest celebrant, a cross, candles, chalice, and paten, and that's about it.

The sanctuary is the center of the weekend experience and the focal point of all of our communication efforts. And, at the same time, it forms a sacred space that aims at being a sign and symbol of heavenly realities. That said, it needs to be worthy of the mystery presented there. That means every element is important and has significance. In turn, that probably means less is going to be more effective and more successful.

We understand many churches are designed and built in historic and elaborate styles with important iconography and rich statuary, all of which must be respected and carefully maintained. But what about:

- chairs that are only needed for weddings or funerals left on the altar as permanent accessories?
- tired or even dead flower arrangements or decorations left from seasons long over?
- banners that are simply old and outdated or altar cloths and linens that are worn, or worse, dirty?

- the choir or music space and all that stuff musicians have (if it is adjacent to your sanctuary)?
- mikes, speakers, and all the attendant wires?

As God reveals himself to Moses and the Israelites, they learn, among other things, that he cares about the details, especially when it comes to the details of worship and worship space.

Carefully consider what your sanctuary is saying.

Is it saying, "The Lord be with you"?

Is it asking, "Lift up your hearts"?

Is it announcing the mystery of faith?

31

LIGHTING IS ARCHITECTURE

Then God said: Let there be light, and there was light. God saw that the light was good. God then separated the light from the darkness.

—Genesis 1:3–4

We tell the story in *Rebuilt* of our decision, several years ago, to move off campus to the Maryland State Fairgrounds for our Christmas Eve celebrations. Among other reasons, this decision was made to better accommodate the crowds that always come at the earliest time available on that day. Among the many lessons that were learned in the process was, unexpectedly, the importance of lighting in good communication.

As we set up a stage for our altar and made all the other necessary arrangements, a friendly maintenance man wandered by and asked us how we were going to light the stage. We hadn't thought about it but instantly realized something would be needed or people wouldn't be able to see very well, given the limited overhead lighting available. The fellow disappeared and eventually returned with a couple of old spotlights he had in storage, and we rigged them up at the last minute.

Tom: The resulting effect was brutal, but it got the job done. The lights were so harsh they gave me a migraine, serving as a painful and unforgettable lesson in the importance of lighting.

In subsequent years, we have come to spend a lot of time on the lighting of our Christmas Eve celebration. Since the setting for the service is the "Cow Palace" (and, yes, it's just as pretty as it sounds), we use minimal lighting, providing only what is needed for safety's sake, and pretty much turn off everything else. Then we strategically illuminate what we want people to see, such as the altar, the choir, and the cross. The lighting transforms an unsightly, old shed into a somewhat dramatic, even elegant, experience.

When we first came to Nativity, the sanctuary and nave were flooded with harsh overhead fluorescent lighting that made everything and everyone look ugly (we irreverently called them the stadium lights). And since it was a seventies-era building (think of lots of dark brown brick), what was being so intensely lit up wasn't worth the effort or expense. Many people would find themselves "counting the bricks" back in the day because the lighting was calling attention to masonry more than anything else.

If you visit our parish these days, you will immediately be struck by how dark our sanctuary is. That's on purpose. We use darkness to hide the building as much as possible and make it go away. Meanwhile, just like our approach at the fairground, we rather dramatically illuminate a few key elements. As the service proceeds, we can even focus the attention of the congregation on what is most important at any given moment, which effectively holds their attention, too.

Lighting communicates mood as well. After Communion, we leave all the altar lights off, except the light on the cross, for a moment of silence and reflection. This intentional use of light has a big impact. Unlike our previous practice, in which everyone was racing for the door following Communion, most people don't move or even make a sound. It is a very powerful experience that's not lost on anyone, and it is all accomplished with light.

Arguably the most beautiful church in the country is the Baltimore Basilica, which was recently meticulously restored. The restoration actually included very few architectural changes. Mostly, it was all about bringing back the light that originally flooded what had become a gloomy, dark space.

Regardless of the style of your church architecture, you can be more deliberate about your lighting, perhaps without any major expense. It's not about brightness or darkness; it's about the most effective use of light in the space you've got. *What* are you illuminating and *why*? What can you change to improve the celebration for your congregation and your guests?

Don't forget, ultimately lighting, not architecture, determines the experience of the building. Lighting is architecture, and it is an important tool for your communication.

One of the first things that ever happened was God being intentional about lighting. It's that important; it's that fundamental.

32
INVEST IN GREAT SOUND

On the seventh day march around the city seven times, and have the priests blow the horns. When they give a long blast on the ram's horns and you hear the sound of the horn, all the people shall shout aloud. The wall of the city will collapse.

—JOSHUA 6:4–5

The weekend is absolutely critical to reaching the lost and getting members on the discipleship path. (See pages 95–97.) We also believe that for the lost, at least initially, the weekend experience rests not on the Eucharist, which they neither appreciate nor understand, but on three critical pillars: *music*, *message*, and *ministers*. Two of those three pillars, in turn, rely on your sound system. If people cannot hear, or must strain to hear, it's going to be difficult for your parish to make the maximum impact you could make or perhaps even the minimum impact you should make. That people can hear is more important than anything in your weekend experience.

So, you need the best sound system you can possibly afford. And what you can afford should be prioritized at the very top of your budget.

Israel's whole approach to the taking of Jericho and the claiming of the promised land is all about sound. So is your weekend experience.

33

THEY HAVE TO SEE, TOO

He threw aside his cloak, sprang up, and came to Jesus. Jesus said to him in reply, "What do you want me to do for you?" The blind man replied to him, "Master, I want to see." Jesus told him, "Go your way; your faith has saved you." Immediately he received his sight and followed him on the way.

—Mark 10:50–52

When we first started visiting and studying some of the most successful evangelical churches, we were surprised by the large video screens that typically flank their sanctuaries. It seemed curious at first, striking us as vaguely inappropriate and largely unnecessary. But here's the thing: we found ourselves inadvertently watching those screens. At some point, it just occurred to us: Why don't we do that, too? Really, why not?

So we did.

At first, we didn't know what we were doing or even really what to do. And to make matters worse, our new technology was constantly malfunctioning. Despite our ignorance, and the missteps that come with trying anything new, not to mention the initial criticism and complaints, we're glad we embraced this technology. For one thing, it's actually becoming more the norm than the exception. Attend Mass in St. Peter's Square or St. Patrick's Cathedral, as well as many new churches around the country, and you will find screens, cameras, and projectors.

But more to the point, they are incredibly helpful tools for communication in a number of ways.

We use our screens to display the lyrics to our worship music. This dispenses with the need for old-fashioned hymnals or the effort and expense of programs. It also gets people's heads up, a much better position to sing. The same is true for the creed and the other Mass parts; when they're on the screens, people tend to participate at a whole new level, and newcomers know what to say and how to join in if they choose to. And the effect is dramatically improved participation.

Most of what we display on the screens are camera shots following the flow of the liturgy itself. The "shots" help the congregation follow the action, especially children who otherwise cannot see beyond the adults in front of them. In fact, they rather demand that people do so.

> **Father Michael:** I remember when we first installed the screens and one person complained. Actually many people complained, but here's what this particular guy said: "I dislike them because they are a distraction." That complaint puzzled me, because, of course, that is exactly what they are not. Unless, that is, you approach Mass as a private devotion or a time to be in your own head, lost in your own thoughts. It is very hard to do that with the screens.

If, in consideration of your church's architecture, if in view of your congregation's culture, or if simply from your own preferences and perspective, it is simply not desirable to use video technology *during* Mass, how about *near* Mass? Screens are an effective place to display your announcements before or after Mass (you can even eventually stop printing a bulletin). They're great to show off photos of parish events or celebrate wins. You can use video screens to thank people and acknowledge their efforts with no expense and little effort. If you have the capacity, you can produce videos to tell your story, go deeper in your message, and even provide testimony of life change and conversion.

Poor Bartimaeus just wants to see. And, if you think about it, when his prayer is answered, the first thing he sees is the Lord. Ultimately, that's our communication, that's our goal: helping people in the pews see the Lord.

34

THE INTERNET IS PROBABLY NOT A PASSING FAD

After this I had a vision of a great multitude, which no one could count, from every nation, race, people, and tongue.

—REVELATION 7:9

We are far from experts on the topic, but in a book on communication we would be remiss if we did not include a chapter on electronic communication and social media. More and more, this is the preferred form of communication, so obviously it should be a growing part of our church communication. In fact, it is probably safe to say we are witnessing one of the major paradigm shifts in the Christian era, and the Church is struggling to catch up.

At the very least, we can acknowledge this different time we are in and put aside our resistance. Every parish can't do everything, but every parish can do some things. If your church is not making use of Twitter, Facebook, and Instagram, if you have no presence in this whole new world that, like it or not, is our world, you are missing out on a huge communication opportunity (perhaps the opportunity of your lifetime). Consider this single, widely reported statistic: the average church using Facebook reaches an audience 166 percent the size of its congregation.

This does not mean the pastor has to master all of it himself, but you need someone or a group of people who are communicating through the medium for you (they can be volunteers). We have parish Facebook and

Twitter accounts, maintained by staff and volunteers, and together they now reach thousands of people *every day*. That means by the end of the week, we have communicated with more people through these mediums than we ever will in our church on even our most well-attended weekend. Learn what types of social media connect to your community. We have found at the moment that Facebook is more popular with our congregation than other social media. At the same time, we are learning that Facebook users are more and more trending older. Social media is changing so fast that this could certainly be different by the time you are reading this book. Be aware that your community, depending on the age and demographics, might be naturally more interested in one or another form of social media.

> **Father Michael:** I have a Twitter account and a blog and use both in my professional capacity as pastor in a consistent way. For Twitter, my current strategy comes down to basically four tweets per day: one from scripture for inspiration, one from some other source for motivation, one from my own daily life and ministry for illustration, and another that's just unexpected or fun. I blog once a week, using that platform to share information with insiders and "reward" them regularly with announcements made before the rest of the congregation gets the news. It's there I also go deeper in discussing church strategy—but not too deep. My posts are always about four hundred words, never more. In just a couple of years, I have developed thousands of followers on Twitter and hundreds of hits weekly on the blog. My consistency has ensured that these numbers continue to grow.

> **Tom:** We also have a service that sends out a daily reflection and prayer via e-mail that we call *Worship Fully*. As well as encouraging daily prayer, it brings a brief message that can be read in a minute or less to reinforce whatever themes we're promoting in our message series or small-group curriculum. Many of our staff members use the same service to keep their sometimes-wide circles of volunteer ministry leaders up to date on events, procedures,

and policies. These distribution systems are a great place for supporting and encouraging our ministers.

It could be said that St. John's vision in Revelation of a great multitude seems to foreshadow the Internet experience. Regardless, God has handed us a powerful tool and expects us to use it.

Call us crazy, but we believe this new thing called the Internet isn't just a passing fad. It's probably here to stay, and yet only 7 percent of churches post a bulletin online. If we aren't leveraging electronic communication in all its forms, then we are missing out in a major way on opportunities to preach the Gospel and spread the Good News.

35

YOU ARE YOUR WEBSITE ... YOU ARE BECOMING YOUR APP

One thing I ask of the LORD; this I seek: to dwell in the LORD's house all the days of my life, to gaze on the LORD's beauty, to visit his temple.

—PSALM 27:4

While your bulletin is old school (and increasingly irrelevant and a waste of paper), your website is more important than ever and a greater opportunity than you realize. The time has come when people will absolutely visit your website *before* they'll ever visit *your church*. And what they see there will determine what they think about your church. You are your website. And because people are more and more relying on their smart phones, tablets, and other mobile devices (more than half of all website traffic now comes from mobile devices), it is critical for your website to be accessible on these devices.

But even more important than a website is a *current* website, one that is consistently updated. It matters not at all that you have a fancy, expensive website with all kinds of bells and whistles. It matters incredibly that you have a website that is *updated weekly*. If you cannot commit to keeping information current, then take down your site until you can. If you have one, keep it up to date and keep it fresh; add new features and pictures from time to time. And by all means, make it attractive.

Beyond that, determine your goals: who you are trying to reach and what you are trying to say. As with any of your other communication tools, if the aim is to reach everyone and say everything, or you have no idea who it could be, it's probably not going to be very effective.

TRY THESE TOOLS

MAKE IT A DESTINATION FOR AN INVITATION

The primary focus of our website is the unchurched Catholics in our community of north Baltimore. After a personal invitation from a parishioner, our website is the second-most important evangelization tool we have. In fact, the two go together, because if people actively consider an invitation to our church, the first thing they're going to do is check out our website. It is the *destination* for the *invitation*. So there has got to be information they're interested in, for example, what to expect if they do come.

MAKE IT A DESTINATION IN ITSELF

The secondary goal of our site is a destination *in itself* for visitors. We have the technology to live stream weekend Masses, but we also make available previously recorded homilies and even other talks, such as small-group materials (help yourself).

MAKE IT A DESTINATION FOR THE PARISH

Of course we also want our site to be helpful and useful to our parishioners (they are not our only audience, or our primary audience, but they are an incredibly important audience). Our website gives them all the information they need, without having to call or stop by the parish office. Our site offers an easy, accessible opportunity to sign up for programs and services, when needed. We now do *all* our sign-ups and registrations online and have begun vigorously promoting online giving.

In the Psalms, David celebrates what he has come to know about the Lord, by spending time with him. Your website can be a place where people in your community who are far from God can get to know you and begin to know him.

It is almost impossible to emphasize enough the importance of your website. But after we have, we need to talk to you about your app. . . .

36

IGNORE DISTRACTIONS

Rising very early before dawn, he left and went off to a deserted place, where he prayed. Simon and those who were with him pursued him and on finding him said, "Everyone is looking for you." He told them, "Let us go on to the nearby villages that I may preach there also. For this purpose have I come."

—Mark 1:35–38

Archbishop Fulton Sheen shared a story about preaching to a community of nuns. Throughout the course of the retreat, one nun consistently sat in the first row, directly in front of the pulpit. Each time he looked up at her, he couldn't help but notice her scowl: there was just no mistaking her displeasure with his message. The woman proved to be such a distraction that he eventually decided to confront her about it and ask her to sit somewhere else. Approaching the sister after one of his talks, the archbishop was surprised to see her whole expression change. Her frown dissolved into a broad smile. She vigorously thanked him for the retreat. What was the disconnect? Turned out, she suffered from chronic back problems that left her in constant pain, thus the grumpy demeanor.

When we step up to the task of communicating, there will always be distractions. People will get up and walk out for no apparent reason. They will talk, text, play with their kids, and gaze off into space as if you had sent them into a coma. With live audiences, distractions are ever present.

And the tendency is to become obsessed with the people who do not seem to be paying attention. We want to figure out why they aren't listening and try to win them back. We can start questioning ourselves or lose our places. But focusing on those distractions will simply weaken our message. They'll keep us from reaching the people who we can reach and moving the people to action who are ready to move.

Ignore the distractions when you are speaking and pretend they are not even there. Stay focused on what you want to communicate and on the people who are with you. (See pages 200–201.)

Beyond that, be proactive about identifying potential distractions before you begin: a mom with a toddler who can't sit still or senior citizens with cell phones they don't know how to mute. All are problems waiting to happen, some of which can be avoided through polite announcements and invitations to better behaviors.

Also, preparation is a useful tool in combatting distractions. The more command you have of your material, the easier it will be to ignore or at least persevere through distractions. (See pages 59–60.)

Mark tells us about the launch of Jesus' public ministry. From the first, he demonstrates an amazing discipline and steadfast refusal to be distracted. In fact, the whole Gospel of Mark is more or less a narration of Jesus' march to the Cross.

Ignore distractions while speaking and develop systems to deal with them as you prepare, and you will go further faster. You can't control people's reactions or the disruptions in your audience. You can only take control of yourself and keep it.

37

FIND COURAGE UNDER FIRE

Rather, after we had suffered and been inso-
lently treated, as you know, in Philippi, we drew
courage through our God to speak to you the
gospel of God with much struggle.

—1 Thessalonians 2:2

Father Michael: I will never forget the first time I mentioned the word "tithe" in a homily. I was met by a woman, immediately after Mass, who wagged her finger at
me menacingly and said, "I never want to hear that word
spoken in this church again." Now I admit, in using it I
hadn't thought much about the word—not to mention
the rather glaring inconsistency that I myself did not tithe
at the time. However, as a result of her criticism, we didn't
mention that word in our church for a very long time. In
fact, the only reason I ever began using it at all was that
Tom threatened to quit if we didn't start preaching it (and
I seriously considered letting him). One intimidating, angry woman kept me from preaching God's Word.

The fear of human beings is a snare. This is especially true when it comes
to communication in churchworld. Everywhere we go to speak we always
get the same question: "If we try your strategies, will anyone complain?" Of
course people will complain, or at least everyone who currently has what

they want in the equation and is afraid your changes will deprive them of it will complain.

We certainly don't want to offend people for the sake of offending them. And we need to avoid turning people off who are far from Christ when they are first coming back to church. However, we also have to accept the fact that sometimes we are going to make people angry, and when they're angry they will probably complain. Some of the complaint will be justified and some will be unfair, but none of it will ever feel very good.

To survive and grow as a communicator, to fulfill the mission God is giving you, requires that you develop courage under fire.

St. Paul knew all about criticism. As a world-class communicator, he stood squarely in the line of fire. He stayed there, and he took it. Draw courage through prayer to speak the Gospel of God. He'll give it to you.

38

IT'S (STILL) THE WEEKEND, STUPID!

"Dismiss the crowd so that they can go to the surrounding villages and farms and find lodging and provisions; for we are in a deserted place here. . . ." Now the men there numbered about five thousand.

—Luke 9:12, 14

Forgive the cliché and the terminology, but if you have read our other books you have heard this before. The weekend is the core "business" and the primary "product" of any church. As we have evaluated our parish and talked with parish leaders elsewhere, we have become more and more convinced of the truth and the utility of this principle. If you also accept this principle, then it naturally follows that the weekend experience is your primary communication tool as a parish. When it comes to communicating, it's still the weekend (sorry about the "stupid" part; it's a long story).

Unchurched people evaluate our parishes based on what they experience on the weekend. They have already stepped out of their comfort zone by coming to church in the first place, and it is our job to reward them for that step and the stretch it represents. If they come and have a decent experience, then there is a chance they will come back again. If they don't, then they won't. That single encounter could be the only chance we get.

Likewise, if we're serious about getting our regulars on a discipleship path and helping them go deeper, the weekend experience is our best, sometimes our only, opportunity to inspire and encourage them to do it.

Beside all that, the weekend serves as the primary statement of what we do, who we are, and what we value. At the Sunday celebration of the Eucharist, we are most fundamentally and authentically who we are. It's also, frankly, where you make your money. Maybe that sounds crass, but it also happens to be true.

TRY THESE TOOLS

REMEMBER THAT IT NEEDS TO BE AN EXPERIENCE

From the first moment people step onto our campus until they leave, we want to communicate that their time with us is an *experience*. Sunday worship is not just about putting an hour in to satisfy God and relieve guilt. Coming to church is not like food shopping or keeping an appointment with the dentist; it's an opportunity to enter into a relationship with the living God and his body, the Church. On any given weekend, our communication includes the homily, the announcements, children's Liturgy of the Word, faith formation, the bulletin, the music, the attitude of the volunteers and staff, and so much more. We want all those elements to create an experience that leads people into a more personal relationship with God and a communal experience of his Church. Every aspect of our effort should communicate this.

MAKE THE EXPERIENCE FLOW

We're not sure where it was decided that great, big cavernous gaps in Mass or yawning silences in between things in the liturgy is a reflection of holiness or an expression of piety. When did starting late or leaving early become an established part of the weekend experience in Catholic parishes? How is it that so many preachers and teachers speak in a way that suggests they're going to go on forever (even if they don't speak very long, they give the impression they will). Regardless of the reasons, the net result is oftentimes lumpy, lumbering experiences that make people, especially unchurched people, anxious and uncomfortable.

From the first, we want to communicate that our parish is a movement, not a monument. It's a movement; that means it's got to move: we want to take people on a journey to the higher things of God before sending them out on a mission to the very basic needs of their brothers and sisters as well as the challenges of their daily lives. To do that, the weekend experience has got to flow, each element leading out of the last, into the next.

MAKE THE EXPERIENCE EXCELLENT

When it comes to the weekend experience, raise up the value of excellence—*excellence*, not perfection. (See pages 123–124.) Excellence is about exceptional or outstanding quality, and even its pursuit honors God and can inspire people.

Sometimes overlooked in the story of the loaves and fishes is the fact that thousands of people followed Jesus into a desolate, isolated setting to hear him preach. They were so taken by the experience that they neglected to make even basic provisions for themselves as night approached. What the disciples fail to understand, and Jesus has to teach them, is that this crowd, this gathering, is an opportunity they must seize.

For us, that's the weekend.

39

AND IT ALL STARTS ON THE PARKING LOT

---⋀---

> But the LORD said to Samuel: Do not judge from his appearance or from his lofty stature, because I have rejected him. God does not see as a mortal, who sees appearance. The LORD looks into the heart.
>
> —1 SAMUEL 16:7

Tom: Not long ago, I took my family to Atlanta to visit my sister Colleen and her family. While in the city, we wanted to do something fun with the kids so we decided to go to the aquarium.

Driving in downtown Atlanta, I experienced a bit of unease. Navigating a city you don't know is stressful. I found a parking lot across the street from the aquarium, and when I pulled up to the gate, the attendant said with a broad, warm Southern accent, "How are you doing, my friend?" Being from the Northeast, I was shocked at the overt friendliness. I paid and pulled into the lot where there was another guy to greet me. Eyeing my oversized Ford Expedition, he said, "You can fit in that spot, my friend. Watch my direction and I'll help you out." He called me his friend, and it seemed as if he meant it. Suddenly, I was so much more relaxed. Before ever setting foot into the aquarium, the experience was already transformative.

Such little details, they seem silly to even recount, except for one thing: I felt great.

After our visit to the aquarium, we headed to Saturday-evening Mass. When we got to the church parking lot, there was a guy in a golf cart who obviously wielded some sort of authority. But he just glared at me and seemed to scowl and sneer as if to say, "You'll never fit that boat in that spot." He watched me try and he definitely made me nervous. It was such a little incident, I probably shouldn't have even noticed, except for one thing: I felt judged.

When people come to Mass on the weekend, every part of their experience communicates to them something about your community, about our God, and what God and your community think about them. Maybe we don't want responsibility like that, but we have it anyway.

TRY THESE TOOLS

HAVE A PARKING TEAM

Communication at Nativity begins first and foremost on our parking lot because, at least in our community, most people drive to church. Consequently, we know our whole weekend message begins there. The parking team, not the homilist, actually starts preaching the Good News. The first experience, and therefore the first communication to the people coming to our church, begins when people drive onto our campus. Our parking team helps guests understand that we are ready and excited to see you.

HAVE A GREETING TEAM

We try to post greeters at our principal entrances for all weekend Masses. Greeters open doors for guests and, of course, greet and welcome them to our church. The greeting team adds words to the wordless welcome of the parking team. They communicate to people that we are glad they've joined us. This is especially important for those who have not been to church in a long time, who assume they are not welcome, and in fact, believe they're being judged. Greeters break down that misconception and help them lower defenses in order to begin to open up to what God wants to say to them.

HAVE A HOST TEAM

After being met by our greeters at the doors, visitors are welcomed by our host team members once inside the church proper (we call it the sanctuary). Hosts help guests find seats and address any special needs, questions, or problems in the sanctuary. They also have the opportunity to carry the conversation forward.

As distinct functions, these are mighty simple things to do, so they are easy to miss. But get them going as a comprehensive team effort and they become so much more than the sum of their parts. Beyond a basic welcome, the parking team, greeters, and hosts all work together to communicate that we're organized. Organization suggests authority and ownership of the ministry and mission of the place. Organization tells those coming to church that we can be trusted. All of this effort at welcoming creates energy and excitement and, in fact, a sense of destination. Church can be a place people really want to be.

God may be able to see beyond a poor first impression, but unchurched people are only human and they often cannot. Our communication begins long before the liturgy does. It begins on the parking lot. It begins with the first impressions guests form as they come onto our campus and into our building.

40

DISPOSE THEM
TO CELEBRATION

So Joshua said to the Israelites, "Come here and listen to the words of the LORD, your God." He continued: "By this you will know that there is a living God in your midst."

—JOSHUA 3:9–10

Before Mass begins, we make announcements, but they are not made by the priest. When the priest is the only voice heard, presiding over Mass, preaching the homily, announcing the announcements, and providing any and all instruction, it subtly (or maybe not so subtly) communicates that the Mass and the church is all about him. It also waters down the impact of his prayer and message since everything he says begins to sound equal.

Our announcements come in the form of a video that currently features two announcers: Kristin is cheerful and friendly and easily makes you smile. Tony is an everyman kind of fellow who deliberately represents that mythical figure we mentioned earlier named "Timonium Tim." He is the quintessential unchurched person that we're trying to reach in our community. When Tim shows up at our church and sees Tony making the announcements, he's very likely to think, "Hey, that guy's like me; I belong here." (See pages 200–201.)

Because of their upbeat style, and a musical soundtrack that accompanies the narrative, our announcements aim at elevating the sense of excitement hopefully already introduced by our host and parking teams. We do not, by the way, think that excitement and enthusiasm are inappropriate attitudes to encourage, as our congregation gathers. Nor are they in the least in opposition to the reverence we owe the Mass (if, by reverence, we mean admiration and awe).

The content of the announcements focuses on what we have come to call "big church." In short, these announcements pertain to general-interest programs and projects that apply to or are open to all. Here we do not convey information about events that have limited appeal or application. Particular announcements can be submitted by anyone but are edited by staff and reviewed by the pastor (that's how important we consider them to be). At the same time, beyond the particulars of the announcements, the message is that there's a lot going on here. It is all carefully scripted with attention to how it will sound to visitors and newcomers, especially the unchurched.

At the end of the announcements, we invite everyone to stand and greet people around them. The invitation is done quickly and simply, and we emphasize it is an invitation and not a command. That, in turn, is capped with a typically vibrant and engaging opening song. When these efforts are successful, we have provided a welcome that has begun to gather and shape a community ready for worship. These opening rituals invite all gathered into a celebration.

God gave Joshua the job of leading Israel into the Promised Land and establishing the nation. That all began boldly and dramatically with the crossing of the Jordan and the fall of Jericho. He knew the importance of a strong start.

As the "General Instruction" to *The Roman Missal* instructs, the purpose of the Introductory Rites is to ensure that the faithful come together to "establish communion" and "dispose themselves . . . to celebrate." That is exactly the message we should be aiming at.

41

NOBODY IS LISTENING TO THE READINGS

When you speak all these words to them, they will not listen to you either. When you call to them, they will not answer you.

—JEREMIAH 7:27

A few years ago, when we first started evaluating the weekend experience at our church, we noticed something quite surprising, even shocking, about the Mass. No one listened to the readings. Really, no one. To confirm this distinct observation, we started informal surveys following Mass, asking people if they could remember anything from the first or second readings. The results confirmed our suspicions (and then some). Don't take our word for it. Try it for yourself.

During the readings, we observed people fussing with their coats or their kids or checking for keys and wallets. Lots of people were using this time to check their phones for texts and tweets or finish conversations suspended as they dashed into Mass. Many people seemed to take this interval to simply close their eyes and catch their breath. Since people in our community tend to come to Mass at the last possible minute (or even late), the readings are, de facto, the time to calm down and settle in.

In fairness, let's face it: the readings can be difficult to tune in to. The lectionary covers a lot of territory and not necessarily in an obviously logical or linear manner. While a biblically literate congregation may be able to recall the context of a given reading, at this point most people in our parish cannot, and the experience remains somewhat inaccessible to them.

Layered on top of that, many of our lectors didn't know what they were reading. They weren't any more familiar with the Bible than the congregation at large. Neither did it help that more than a few of them were unprepared and clearly, sometimes painfully, unfamiliar with what they were reading. Oh, and most of them didn't know how to use the microphone either. Some of them just didn't seem to care, almost as if they approached the task not as ministry but as entitlement.

In the last few years, we have worked to help overcome these problems. Of course, this process began by acknowledging we *had* a problem.

Now, we have only a select few who serve as lectors, and we make no apologies about that. Just because you want to be a lector doesn't qualify you to be a lector at our parish. You actually have to have talent. And then, you've got to prepare and practice. (See pages 59–60 and 63–65.) Meanwhile, through our preaching and small-groups teaching efforts we're working on the biblically literate part for our lectors, as well as for the larger congregation.

The unhappy task of announcing the impending fall of Jerusalem and subsequent exile of the nation fell to the prophet Jeremiah. Unfortunately, no one was listening, as the Lord had advised the prophet to anticipate. At least *initially* no one was listening. Knowing that up front was a powerful tool for what came to be Jeremiah's very effective communication.

42

MAKE AN OFFERING

⌃

"And do you not remember, when I broke the
five loaves for the five thousand, how many
wicker baskets full of fragments you picked
up?" They answered him, "Twelve."

—Mark 8:18–19

The Roman Missal explains, "The faithful express their participation by *making an offering*, bringing forward bread and wine for the celebration of the Eucharist and perhaps other gifts to relieve the needs of the Church and of the poor."

When it came to what this actually looked like in our parish, we gave it absolutely no consideration whatsoever. The established practice prevailed. To the accompaniment of typically dreary music, our ushers performed a sort of military maneuver. They marched down the aisles, shouldering baskets attached to long handles that were thrust before unsuspecting parishioners as quickly as possible. The drill was actually a contest to see who could complete his section fastest. After that, both the ushers and the collection disappeared—the money to be counted, the ushers for a coffee break.

As we started to become more mindful and deliberate about stewardship and giving at our parish, an obvious thought occurred to us: Why not approach this moment as something beyond just taking up a collection or passing a basket? Why not try to communicate the idea of an offering?

First of all, we got rid of the baskets entirely, which were old, dirty, and beaten up, and went with small, good-looking canvas bins ($6.99 at Target). Instead of merely appearing and disappearing at the hand of another, the bins are passed from person to person, allowing everyone to participate in the exercise. While the contents of the bins, collected by the host team, are actually deposited directly into a safe (for reasons of security), a larger bin symbolizing the whole offering is brought to the altar in the offertory procession. It remains there until after the Communion Rite. During the offering, celebrant and ministers offer a silent prayer for those participating in the offering through their gifts and tithes. A few times each year we take a minute before the offering to explain its significance as well as the programs and services it makes possible.

The miracle of the feeding of the five thousand begins as an offering. The apostles give what they can give and Jesus provides the rest. Far exceeding the seemingly impossible, the result is profound abundance and deep blessing.

It is easy to overlook or brush past the transition that is the offertory, but it is crucial to seize this rich opportunity for precise communication. It is, in fact, an opportunity to express what is at the very heart of the Eucharist itself: an offering that becomes a sublime exchange yielding profound abundance and deep blessing.

43

COMMUNE
AT COMMUNION

Every day they devoted themselves to meeting together in the temple area and to breaking bread in their homes. They ate their meals with exultation and sincerity of heart, praising God and enjoying favor with all the people. And every day the Lord added to their number those who were being saved.

—ACTS 2:46–47

The whole of Jesus' life led inexorably to the Cross. The Cross casts its shadow over everything that happened from Simeon's prophecy to Mary at the Presentation of Jesus in the Temple through the Lord's discourse to the disciples at the Last Supper. Step by step, his life was a journey toward Calvary. In a wonderful pattern that reflects this plan, everything at Mass leads toward the great Eucharistic Prayer and Holy Communion.

Communion is about mystery, solemnity, and a growing relationship with Jesus Christ who humbles himself to become flesh and blood for us in bread and wine. It is intimate and personal, but it is not private. It is corporate and meant to strengthen the community into which God calls us at Baptism. That's why we approach this time in our weekend experience with great care, thoughtfully aware of what it is we're communicating.

At Nativity, we do this through music. For the Communion procession, we choose music that is beautiful and easy to sing (since people tend to stop singing when they have to do something like stand up and form a line). We look for music that softly soars as we receive a gift that is meant to be personally and communally transformative.

We also tend to this most important part of the liturgy by the simplicity of our actions. We have worked hard to alleviate complication when it comes to the movements of our Eucharistic ministers and ushers during the Communion Rite. What we found in place when we came here was all so thoughtlessly, needlessly, complicated that we came to call it the "dance of the seven veils." Our current procedures are all straightforward and simple as can be. Neither is there anything else going on. Communion is what's happening.

We communicate carefully through subtle stuff, too, which we hope is effectively communicating that Communion is not the end; it is not the conclusion of the service. We keep the sanctuary doors closed, bring the music to a gentle conclusion, and then, very deliberately, settle into a moment of silence. It all unmistakably communicates that this isn't over folks. Over time, these practices have built a culture in which most people (not all for sure, but most) stay through the dismissal.

The most remarkable aspect of the new community of Christ followers we read about in the Acts of the Apostles was their unparalleled sense of communion and fellowship. Everyone noticed it, and more and more people wanted to be a part of it.

At the heart of our weekend experience is the Communion Rite. We must be very careful what we are communicating here because this communion is quite literally rebuilding Christ's Church.

44

LAND THE PLANE

As they were looking on, he was lifted up, and a cloud took him from their sight.

—Acts 1:9

In our current approach, after Communion comes a gentle end to the music followed by a moment (a moment, not minutes) of silence. Everyone at our place seems to appreciate that moment of silence as long as they're not dreading that it's stretching out into minutes of silence. The prayer after Communion brings this moment, and the Communion Rite, to a close. In many parishes, announcements are read at this point. That's what we also did when we first came here. The celebrant would essentially read the bulletin, or at least major highlights on the theory, which was correct, that no one actually read the bulletin itself. Perhaps it was this custom, in turn, that fueled the mass exodus we witnessed following Communion each week.

We make our announcements *before* Mass. (See pages 101–102.) After Communion comes something we've found ourselves calling "endnotes." These notes are not announcements. Instead, given by various members of our staff, they serve another purpose, in fact, several purposes.

First: We want to show that the parish staff is not just our pastor; there is depth of leadership at the church, and it is a team effort.

Second: We use this moment as another opportunity to greet guests and visitors and tell them one more time we are glad they came. So we will say something along the lines of, "If you are not a church person, not a religious person, if this was your first time in church in a long time or first time ever, if you are only here because someone begged you, bribed you, or promised you brunch, welcome. We're glad you're here. We want to be a church for people who don't like church." This also serves as a gentle reminder to our parishioners that part of their commission in the coming week is to be on the lookout for unchurched friends and family they can invite to church.

> **Tom:** I'm often the one to make this announcement, and countless times following Mass parishioners will come to me and say, "I'm inviting someone to Mass next Sunday. Please, please, please, make sure you say that for them."

Third: We sum up the homily. We remind people what our basic message was and the challenge offered to them in the message. Basically, we're giving them a bottom line that they can carry with them out of Mass and into their week.

To that end, we plug a single step people can take away: putting the message into action, doing something on Monday in light of their experience on Sunday, or participating in an upcoming event at the church that supports the message. Sometimes the events are important steps we want people to take and so we emphasize those in endnotes.

- In a series on worry, we gave away a prayer card and invited people to take it home and pray whenever they found themselves worrying.
- In a series called "Tough Love," we encouraged members to attend one of a series of breakouts we were offering to go deeper with relationship issues: a married life "date night," a caregivers' workshop, and a workshop on how to talk to your teens about sex.
- In an evangelization series, we provided invitation cards (inviting unchurched people to church) that parishioners could use to invite guests.

> **Father Michael:** Whenever possible, we also want people to leave laughing, especially if the message was challenging or convicting. We try to stay away from the merely shticky or the simply silly. Perhaps we'll play off a story I've shared or a comment made about, say, pop culture that lends itself to sardonic mischaracterization. Sometimes Brian or Chris, or other younger staff members, will make fun of me in some charming way. This brings me down off of any pedestal that people have placed me on and

makes the whole message we're communicating more human and accessible. Typically we are self-deprecatory as a way of showing people we take our message seriously, not ourselves.

Tom: By the way, the priesthood belongs on a pedestal, but it's good for Michael to step down from it once in a while. We're not trying to blur proper boundaries or confuse roles; we're just having fun. Also, some may say the humor is superfluous, but so is all of creation. God invented humor, and when we use it to connect people to Christ, it is well used. If people leave church laughing, there is a good chance they will want to come back.

Following his death and the Resurrection, Jesus didn't just leave the disciples hanging. He returned, giving them further and final instruction. But he also didn't linger. He brought things full circle and then gave his followers the ending they needed.

45

PROGRESS IN SOLEMNITY

> Then David came dancing before the Lord with abandon, girt with a linen ephod. David and all the house of Israel were bringing up the ark of the Lord with shouts of joy and sound of horn. As the ark of the Lord was entering the City of David, Michal, daughter of Saul, looked down from her window, and when she saw King David jumping and dancing before the Lord, she despised him in her heart.
>
> —2 Samuel 6:14–16

Even the saddest funeral will have a moment of laughter; even the most joyous wedding has a poignant, tearful time, too. We like to say that the best experiences, the ones we welcome the most and return to most often, have a landscape to them. They take us somewhere; they progress.

In Catholic worship, singing is understood as the most solemn form of prayer. The principle of progressive solemnity teaches that since not every part of every Mass can reasonably be sung, preference ought to be given to the more important liturgical parts or elements. In fact, a hierarchy is suggested within the liturgy itself, by liturgical norms, and also in the course of the liturgical year.

We have no intention of entering into a liturgical debate; that's just too dangerous. But we would like to make one, slender point that dabbles in the liturgical. What if our whole approach to the weekend experience was a *progressive solemnity*?

Probably ever since the Second Vatican Council's reform of the liturgy, there has been a push and a pull, back and forth between guardians of the sacred and solemn and advocates of the warm and welcoming (not to say fuzzy). But what if we just called this a false choice, a needless argument, an unfortunate and unnecessary distraction and choose *both* instead. What if we meet people where they are and actually help them progress toward the profound solemnity that is the Mass of the Roman Rite?

By the time people hit our campus on Sunday morning, they have already had a struggle (if not a battle) to get the kids dressed and out the door; maybe there have been drama and tears, too. Even for people without kids, there's the hassle of overcommitted schedules and traffic. However devoted or well intentioned they may be, very few people actually show up recollected and ready for Mass. Greeting them in a friendly and even fun way begins to change the tone of where they are and brings them to another place.

Our weekend Masses are preceded by video announcements that are intentionally cheery and sometimes quite funny. Some would argue this is a place for quiet prayer and preparation, and we agree that it is, for some parishioners (we have a chapel for that purpose). But for the vast majority of people who are coming to our parish, they're not ready for quiet prayer yet. Just as they need transitional spaces, which they find in our café and other gathering places before entering the sanctuary, they also need transition *time* back to churchworld. Most of the people coming to church on any given weekend haven't given it a thought for about a week. (See pages 101–102.)

Our opening music is almost always buoyant and engaging (though toned down in Lent) with the express intent of gathering together what is only a random collection of people into a *congregation*.

Conversely, during the Liturgy of the Eucharist we sing the acclamations in traditional Latin Gregorian chant. This solemn chant stands in stark and strikingly beautiful contrast to much of the rest of our music. We have found that it powerfully underscores the *different moment* that the congregation has entered at this point in the Mass. It works for the same reason bells do at the consecration and sometimes incense, too. Lights are focused on the action at the altar, and silence punctuates everything during the Liturgy of the Eucharist. All of this unmistakably tells everyone, this is the heart and soul of the whole experience.

On the other side of the Eucharist is celebration and motivation. It is meant to be a high energy send-off.

King David's celebration as he brought the Ark of the LORD to Jerusalem did not at all reflect the highly formal worship that would characterize the Temple liturgy to come. And neither did everyone appreciate his approach (boy oh boy, we know how that feels). But David was successfully leading the vast majority of people into worship of the living God. That was the point. The same is true for us on the weekends. We're not advocating any particular liturgical procedures or musical styles, but we do hold firm to the principle behind our choices. When it comes to *your* parish's weekend communication beginning to end, first and last, *you* have the opportunity to take people on a journey into the realm of higher things.

Part III
ABOUT YOUR DELIVERY

46

IT'S THEATER

———————/\———————

> The city was filled with confusion and the people rushed with one accord into the theater, seizing Gaius and Aristarchus, the Macedonians, Paul's traveling companions. Paul wanted to go before the crowd, but the disciples would not let him.
>
> —ACTS 19:29–30

Both of us performed in college theater, and we both enjoyed it. Live presentations create energy and excitement, as well as tension and drama. If you've ever performed on stage, you know the feeling, too.

Theater, like sports, requires you to work on a team, be accountable to the other team members, and really rely on them. Good theater engages the audience, creates an experience for them apart from the daily grind, and adds value to their lives by influencing, maybe even radically changing, lives.

We know that in churchworld suggesting that the Church is a business is distasteful to people because it's *not* a business. Equally offensive, or perhaps more so, would be the assertion that "church is theater" because it's not theater. Church is not theater; it is the Body of Christ. Mass is not theater; it is the Word and Sacrament of the living God. We'll say it again just so we cannot possibly be misquoted.

Church is *not* theater. Period.

(But, it *kinda* is.)

Consider we're talking about presentations before live audiences, most of which require teamwork and rehearsal, or at least some kind of preparation. And it is definitely meant to influence and change people's views and behaviors, hopefully even their lives. And what we are communicating concerns the greatest drama in the history of the world, the most important story ever told. The story of our salvation is a drama. Shouldn't our communication of it be at least a little dramatic?

One of the most common myths when it comes to preaching and teaching in churchworld is that if it looks or smells like a performance, then the message is somehow compromised. If it's entertaining and engaging, then somehow it must be inauthentic or, worse, unorthodox. We'd certainly agree that there is a subtle line between self-aggrandizing performance that gets in the way of the message and compelling communication. Jesus' own teaching was evidently mesmerizing. He was a master storyteller, with stories full of plot twists and surprise endings. It is easy to imagine him speaking in different voices to give life to his different characters. He could be funny; he could be inspiring; and he could bring on a fiery condemnation now and then, too.

To effectively preach and teach, you must be faithful and authentic, motivated, and moved by a burden to communicate the Gospel of Jesus Christ. But don't ignore the element of performance you are operating in and the stage you stand on.

The life of Paul, as recounted in Acts of the Apostles, is full of drama, nowhere more apparent than during his eventful third mission journey. In fact, on that trip his preaching had so much impact it sparked a riot in the city of Ephesus, played out, literally, in a theater.

When it comes to your communication, you should not miss out on the drama you are a part of. Just don't start any riots.

47

EVEN THE
BAD NEWS IS GOOD

⌃

I came so that they might have life and have it
more abundantly.

—John 10:10

Recently, Kathleen, a friend of ours, shared that her daughter, a college
freshman, is not going to church, even though she was thoroughly engaged
at our parish throughout her high school years and remains so when back
home on vacation. Why? Well, she doesn't attend because the experience
of Mass on her campus is beyond boring and bad; it's offensive. The priest
regularly uses the homily time to actually yell at the students for drinking,
getting drunk, sleeping around, sleeping in, and not coming to church on
Sunday mornings. Of course, the guilty parties, whomever they might be,
are probably not present to hear his rants. Only the innocent are punished.
Julie doesn't even drink, but thanks to the experience of that church, she
doesn't go to church at college either.

We are stewards of a message that is good news. The basic and the
ultimate message of our faith is that God loves us, despite what we have
done wrong. We have and hold good news that sin and selfishness are not
the last word; life is stronger than death, and loves wins no matter what.
All good news.

Sometimes, though, it is true that in order to deliver the good news,
we have to deliver bad news, too. Sometimes we have to challenge people
to take steps they don't want to take, do things they don't want to do, form
habits they don't feel like forming. Sometimes we need to point out sin in
people's lives, sin they might like or want to hold onto. We especially have

tough challenges we must meet when it comes to giving, serving, and praying. The reality is that there is greed, selfishness, and lots of other hateful tendencies in human nature. In order to share good news, we sometimes have to help people understand the bad news of their sin. That's the reality of communicating a prophetic message.

Every once in a while though, we get the feeling certain communicators just enjoy bad news: the preacher who doesn't just preach the biblical truth of hell but actually sounds as if he relishes the idea of God sending people there; the talk-radio host who amplifies or fabricates setbacks in the ongoing cultural wars to send his listeners into hysterics; or the blogger who only writes or tweets overblown negative assessments of the world around us or the Church we share.

From whatever perspective you're communicating, it's easy to tell people what it is they already believe and want to hear anyway. Likewise, it is not very difficult to communicate in a manner that judges, condemns, or at the very least, excludes people. It can be fun to wield a sledgehammer, especially if the people we're bashing aren't even present.

It is more challenging, and much more effective, to speak with love that in turn leads to life change. Don't shy away from difficult subjects when and where they should be addressed; just do it in a way people can hear. For example:

- By all means teach about the necessity of tithes and offerings, by teaching first of all about the rewards of generosity.
- Do not neglect the Church's teaching on sexuality, but perhaps begin by communicating the blessings and benefits of purity, even beyond past failures.
- We're not saying let people off the hook when it comes to mission and ministry service, but how about presenting it in a way that's actually accessible for them.

The message of the Gospel, as St. John reminds us in the words of our Savior, is all about life: our life, the lives of our families and friends, and the life of the world. When approaching difficult issues, remember that Jesus challenges us in order to help us live more successful, more abundant lives.

Guilt and bad feelings don't attract people to church and neither do they work for life change. Even the most difficult of his teachings, to take up the cross, is a message of life and love.

So, it should always sound like good news, right?

48

PRESENTATION TRUMPS CONTENT

So Elijah said to the people, "I am the only remaining prophet of the LORD, and there are four
hundred and fifty prophets of Baal. Give us two
young bulls. Let them choose one, cut it into
pieces, and place it on the wood, but start no
fire. . . . You shall call upon the name of your
gods, and I will call upon the name of the LORD.
The God who answers with fire is God."

—1 KINGS 18:22–24

A friend shared a story about seeing a woman whose car was on fire. He
was stopped at a traffic light, and across the intersection, he could see fire
coming out of her engine. A driver in the next lane noticed the fire, too,
and tried to provide warning by running toward her car with his hands
waving wildly. The woman, perhaps thinking he was crazy, quickly locked
her car doors and sped off. While the man had some very pertinent information, the woman wasn't open to hearing it because of how it was
presented to her.

Tom: As a political science major in college, one semester I had two required classes back to back: "Politics in the
American South" and "The Modern US Presidency." Southern history had always interested me, and I especially
looked forward to that class. And yet, week after week,
those seventy-five minutes seemed like the longest of my

life. Meanwhile, the presidency class proved unexpectedly fascinating. The professor told stories, added color and
texture to the issues presidents faced, and even "got into
character" from time to time with different voices and
mannerisms. And as a result, those seventy-five minutes
seemed to fly by. While I often found myself daydreaming
in the one class, I was fully engaged in the other.

Presentation matters. It matters in cooking. It matters in movies and
plays. It matters in teaching and preaching, too. Presentation, not content,
determines interest. Why is that?

The reason may be that God cares about it. Look at the beauty of the
stars in the sky, the colors of the trees in autumn, and the artistry of a single
snowflake. God created the world in a beautiful, wondrous way. Any kind
of excellence in presentation becomes a reflection of that and, as a conse-
quence, is relevant and attractive to us.

In your presentation, are there people and personalities you can bring
to life? You can add flavor with stories and illustrations, details, and humor,
which you can sculpt and shape and "speak into life." (See pages 61–62.)
Be playful and have fun with your communication. Delight in your message as God delights in creation. If you are enjoying the presentation, your
audience will, too, and that means they will be more likely to hear and care
about your main point.

The prophet Elijah places a clear choice before the people, marking the
distinct difference between false gods and the living Lord God of Israel. But he sets his argument in the context of a fascinating and dramatic
presentation. The people are convinced and converted. The life-changing,
world-changing message we are charged to communicate deserves nothing
less than our very best effort at presentation.

49

PERFECTION IS A PATH

For we know partially and we prophesy partially, but when the perfect comes, the partial will pass away.

—1 Corinthians 13:9–10

Perfectionism is a personality trait characterized by the pursuit of the flawless, an ongoing attempt to achieve the unattainable.

> **Tom:** I often say I was a much better father before I ever had kids. The birth of my son Max woke me up to the reality that I didn't know what I was doing when it came to parenting. Of course, if I had waited until I was ready to be a parent, I would never have had children. One is never ready for parenthood. You never have it all together. You will make mistakes and you will make them over and over again. They inevitably spring from character flaws, lack of skill, and basic misunderstanding of the role itself.

The same is true in communication. However much you prepare and practice, you are never completely prepared; you're not really ready. There is always room for improvement. Perfection is a myth. Self-improvement is not, but the only way to improve your communication is to communicate imperfectly. The only way to get better as a speaker is to step up to speak. Prepare as much as you can, practice every chance you get, with the knowledge that it's never going to be perfect. (See pages 59–60 and 63–65). In fact, missteps or mistakes in your presentation can make you more approachable, and your message less intimidating.

The same goes for your personal flaws and shortcomings. When appropriately acknowledged or exposed, they make you more credible. In fact, go ahead and point them out, because when you do you'll connect with your audience at a whole new level.

It might even win you influence. (See pages 10–13.)

Perfectionism and worry about being perfect are the enemies of good communication. In fact, it can have a paralyzing effect leaving you with little from which to effectively communicate.

St. Paul understood what we often do not: this side of heaven only God's Word is perfect. Your communication of it is not, but never let that stop you. Perfection isn't the goal. Perfect isn't even a goal at all, it's a path for our preaching and teaching.

50

DO EXEGESIS (ON YOUR COMMUNITY)

With that, Joseph hurried out, for he was so overcome with affection for his brother that he was on the verge of tears. So he went into a private room and wept there.

—GENESIS 43:30

One of the greatest compliments you can receive when communicating is to hear someone say, "I felt as if you were speaking directly to me." In a crowd of dozens or hundreds of people, it means you have connected one-on-one with someone you might not even know.

It's a major goal of our communication that people feel as if we're talking *to them* and that the message of the Gospel is *for them*—because it is.

As human beings, we often know what we are supposed to do. Typically our problem is not that we don't know what to do; our problem is we don't *want* to do it. We need to be reminded and encouraged in making solid choices and right decisions. It isn't enough for us to know intellectually the good, the true, and the beautiful; we need to connect emotionally as well. If we ignore how our audience is feeling as well as the emotional pull of our message, we simply will not move our people toward life change.

God created us as emotional beings. He designed emotions to help drive us to act and move, ultimately in his direction. When we feel sorrow, it is easier for us to repent. When we feel grateful, it is easier for us to give and be generous. When we feel the reality of our loneliness or need for community, it is easier for us to join a small group. Using emotions is not manipulation if it taps into the truth of our situation.

Great communicators connect with the hearts of their audience as well as their heads. To successfully rebuild your message and effectively communicate the Gospel, we absolutely must connect with our audience emotionally.

And to do that, you have to do homework, a kind of exegesis of your community, a critical evaluation of who they are and what is going on.

TRY THESE TOOLS

PROBE THE LOCAL CULTURE

Understanding your community means getting to know how they spend their time, how they spend their money, what they like, and what they're like. The best way to do that is to live in your parish. Shop where your people shop, eat where they eat, follow local sports and other programing for the kids of your neighborhood.

CONSIDER VARIOUS LIFE EXPERIENCE

Think, for instance, what a message on money might mean for high school students, collegians, young working adults, parents, and the elderly. The same topic will hit each of those groups differently on an emotional level. If you acknowledge that, they will be much more inclined to listen.

Also, not everyone is going to agree with you. You can actually use that to your advantage. When you voice your audience's disagreements with your message, you show that you really do understand where they are coming from and you make an instant and easy emotional connection. They feel as if you understand them and so will give you a hearing. By pointing out their arguments, you help disarm them, maybe even change their minds.

ASK YOURSELF, WHAT MAKES THEM HAPPY AND WHAT DO THEY FEAR?

When we argue from ideas, we lose. When we argue from the point of view of helping people achieve success and fulfillment, we win. Our culture is not on a truth quest. Maybe you don't like that, but it is so. We are on a happiness quest, and if we are to influence people for Christ, we must know what makes them happy, at least what they think makes them happy. Then we can then connect those desires to the God who wills our ultimate good and happiness; then we've got an argument people want to listen to.

In our community, for instance, sports command the culture and rule the calendar. It does absolutely no good whatsoever to wish it were otherwise or demand that it be different. We may as well wish that our people would speak a different language. Instead, to be effective communicators for our parish, we have to grow in our understanding and appreciation of exactly how and why our people hardwire their happiness to lacrosse and football.

Knowing your community also means knowing their fears. What do the people you're preaching to or teaching fear? The most common fears in Timonium include economic misfortune, job instability, and loss of physical health. Our parishioners are haunted by fear for their children's safety and well-being. But probably most of all, they fear failure.

Genesis tells, at length, the beautiful story of a beautiful man named Joseph. Despite many injustices perpetrated on him, he remained steadfast toward God and kept his heart free from anger. And the Bible tells us that the blessing of the Lord remained with him. Later, when he has an opportunity to share that blessing with his brothers, he does. In fact, he saved their lives. Such charity was possible because he knew them and, literally, where they were coming from. His understanding helped change everything; it's the same for your message, too.

51

SERIES ARE SIMPLER

Jacob called his sons and said: "Gather around, that I may tell you what is to happen to you in days to come."

—Genesis 49:1

When we began studying healthy, growing churches, we learned that the message, what Catholics call the homily, was an important part of their weekend services—very important. We also learned they organized their messages into series—also very important.

A message series is about taking a specific topic and, over a number of weeks, developing it, going deeper. The churches we've studied also packaged or branded each of their series with a specific look and style that communicated the tone and theme of the series with the aim of stimulating interest. The brand is subsequently promoted on their website and through social media. In other words, each series has its own mini-marketing campaign.

> **Father Michael:** One Advent a few years back, we finally gave the idea a try. I preached all of the weekend Masses, regardless of who was celebrating Mass. We also made sure the Children's Liturgy of the Word was aligned with the series theme. And I've got to tell you, I loved it.

For one thing, a message series actually makes it easier to put together a homily from week to week. When you're in a series, you don't have to come up with all new material every week, neither do you have to constantly start from a blank slate. You've already determined your topic as well as the general direction in which you're headed. For anyone who has the responsibility to preach week after week, the advantage this provides cannot be overstated. It also makes so much sense when it comes to the lectionary cycles and the liturgical seasons, which beautifully, perfectly lend themselves to series; they *are* series in themselves, of course.

Here's another reason we like message series: we think one of the main goals of a message is simply to start a conversation. If we get people talking about the message on the car ride home, around the dinner table, or at sporting events, those are huge wins for us. If a single message can get the conversation started, a series will keep it going. In turn, the conversation has the potential to change and transform people's thinking, which eventually leads to changed lives.

For instance, although a stand-alone, single Sunday message on stewardship is probably not going to change many people's minds about giving, a series definitely has that potential.

Message series also help move the parish in a disciplined direction. If you are clear and consistent through a series, and it is reflected in the children's and student programs as well as your small group curriculum, there will be outcomes that impact and change your whole parish. (See pages 163–165.) We've seen that over and over again when it comes to what we want people to do: giving, serving, small groups, daily prayer, and confession. Now, in our planning, we'll ask the questions: how do we want *people* to change, and how do we want the *parish* to change as a result of a series?

When it came time, Jacob gathered his family and shared with them the plan, the master plan. It was a plan charting the course forward for a family that would become a tribe, that would become a nation, and that would change the world.

The simplest and entirely cost-free thing you can do to unite your parish and powerfully move your mission forward to the future God has in view for you is to preach messages in a series. Think of it as your master plan.

52

AVOID THE
CURSE OF KNOWLEDGE

The LORD God gave the man this order: You are free to eat from any of the trees of the garden except the tree of knowledge of good and evil. From that tree you shall not eat; when you eat from it you shall die.

—GENESIS 2:16–17

A few years ago we had an idea to form prayer teams to pray with parishioners after Mass. In the typical weekend homily, we know we sometimes stir people's emotions or even intentionally bring them to a place where they have to face their own baggage or issues. Rather than just send them out the door to deal with their issues by themselves, we wanted to try to support them. So, we identified a few key people we thought had the right heart, as well as the spiritual maturity, to provide this service. We described our plan to them as a way of being more *pastoral* to the people in our pews and some of the details about how this new ministry would work. After a short presentation, we asked the group, all committed members of our church, if they had any questions. One person raised his hand, "What do you mean by being 'pastoral'?" All the others nodded. They all had the same question.

In churchworld, we have all sorts of terms we've learned in seminary or some other academic setting, which nobody in the pews knows: catechumenate, transubstantiation, eschatology, and so forth. Worse still, we take these specialized, rarified words and make acronyms out of them: RCIA, GRIM, USCCB, and the like. Just take a survey in your parish of how many people can decode RCIA. There is nothing wrong with that at a professional level for churchpeople. Every profession and every field of study forms its own language for its own use. But we make a mistake when we take for granted that parishioners and others know them as well.

We have all been in the situation where a professional started using words we didn't understand. To avoid looking stupid, we nodded in apparent agreement, but in reality, they'd lost us. We can easily do the same thing with the people in the pews. We lose them if we rely on terms they don't understand.

This mistake in communication has been called the curse of knowledge. To effectively communicate, we obviously need to know what we are talking about, but it can become a curse when we assume our audience has the same knowledge we have. We've got to be on guard about what we assume our parishioners know and even more vigilant when it comes to people new to our parish. Be very careful about such assumptions. The very things you assume people know, they often don't know.

In the creation narrative, along with everything else he creates, God creates law in the form of a command he gives Adam. The law provided a better way to be in the garden, with humanity living under divine authority. With their violation of God's law, they bring a curse upon themselves. Our communication efforts can be diminished and our credibility as communicators eroded if we are not attentive to that curse.

53

DON'T SAY TOO MUCH

In praying, do not babble like the pagans, who think that they will be heard because of their many words. Do not be like them.

—MATTHEW 6:7–8

An experiment was undertaken in a supermarket regarding marketing of various fruit jams. Two displays, promoting the same exact brand of the jam, were set up in two different locations in the same store. One display offered twenty-four different flavors of jam; the other had only six. Which display sold more? If you've read the title of this chapter, you might already have a guess. The display offering fewer choices quickly sold out, while sales from the larger display were sluggish. Upon review, the marketers arrived at the conclusion that the multiplication of choices was confusing and perhaps just overwhelming to potential customers.

We live in the Information Age. Every day we are assaulted with tweeting and texting, social media, twenty-four-hour news cycles, cable TV, and talk radio; the list goes on and on. Ironically, there is a growing awareness that even though we have all this information, we are more and more unlikely to do anything with it. The sheer amount of what is available can actually confuse us. And the more confused we become, the less likely we are to act. We can be overwhelmed.

How many times have you been to a hotel that has one of those brochure displays for area attractions? Perhaps you glance at one or two and then give up. There are just too many. How many times have you turned on the TV, taken a look at the menu of options, and ended up spending more time trying to decide what to watch than actually watching anything? How many times have you gotten to the mall, paused to consider the vast expanse of stores, and just left? (Okay, maybe that one is just a guy thing, but you get the idea.)

Because of this, we yearn for simplicity in our culture, and the same is true in our parish.

We know a parish that boasts that they have ninety-three ministries. Some time ago, they had a ministry fair to recruit new volunteers for all those ministries. After Masses, many parishioners wandered through the parish hall—perhaps out of curiosity or courtesy—but very few actually volunteered. Organizers were surprised by the lack of response, but they shouldn't have been. It was no reflection on their parishioners' level of commitment. The culprit was simply too many choices. From time to time, we also host a similar ministry fair, and typically we offer only four to five ministry choices. The response is always solid and encouraging.

Jesus' instructions in prayer apply to all our communication. Regardless of your message, don't overburden your audience or congregation with too much information, too many facts, or an array of choices. Don't say too much.

54

LET IT FLOW

It shall come to pass I will pour out my spirit upon all flesh. Your sons and daughters will prophesy, your old men will dream dreams, your young men will see visions. Even upon your male and female servants, in those days, I will pour out my spirit. I will set signs in the heavens and on the earth.

—JOEL 3:1–3

Time is both objective and relative. Sixty seconds is sixty seconds. Sixty minutes is sixty minutes. You can't create or destroy time. But time is also very relative; when we're having fun, life speeds up and time flies. And we also all know times when the clock seems to slow down, when minutes feel like hours and hours like days. Unfortunately, many liturgical celebrations fall into this latter category.

When it comes to our communication, the *relative* experience of time is far more important than the *objective* time itself. We've all heard arguments in favor of specific time limits for homilies. We think such ideas might tend to miss precisely this point: if you are a gifted speaker, people will be left wanting more at the twenty-minute mark; on the other hand, listening to a bad preacher preach for ten minutes is going to seem like a brush with eternity.

Perhaps the key ingredient to using time to your advantage is what we'll call *flow*. If your message sounds smooth and feels as if it's moving, you've got flow and it goes a long way toward engaging your audience and keeping them from turning to their phones. If you've got flow, you can communicate more effectively for longer, and you can cover more ground.

Flow overcomes the objective reality of time and creates another reality, a subjective reality.

Flow is about your transitions. This is where it is easy to lose momentum, to interrupt what pace you've already established, as well as confuse your audience. Moving from your introduction to the body of your message or from the body to application and conclusion can be very awkward, even disruptive. Transitions are very important, and you probably need to put a lot more time into them than you think. Definitely don't leave them till the last minute or treat them as an afterthought.

Flow is also about the modulation of your voice, the mastery of speed, and knowing when and how to slow down, even stop, allowing silence to provide emphasis and punctuation.

Think, too, about the energy and emotional health you bring to your presentation. That also impacts your flow.

A wonderful vision of the future is described by the prophet Joel. In it, among other things, amazing communication and revelation can be expected. It is all a gift of the Holy Spirit, and you could call it flow. Flow is sort of what the Spirit does. Good communication is all about flow. So pray for it.

55

HELP THEM FOLLOW YOU

When the chief priests and the Pharisees heard his parables, they knew that he was speaking about them.

—MATTHEW 21:45

No one wants to be preached to. As Christian communicators, we need to come to terms with that simple fact.

Nobody wants to be preached to, and very few people want to be told what to do. Good preaching and teaching should engage people in a conversation (see pages 166–168), take them on a journey (see pages 194–196), and form bonds with the listener (see pages 200–201). But, at its core, it needs to do something else, too: subtly, very subtly, it needs to build an argument.

All spiritual change and growth requires assent of the mind and often begin there. That means we are in the business of changing people's thinking. St. Paul says, as Christian communicators, we're destroying arguments and strongholds of thought in the minds of our listeners and creating fresh ways of thinking (2 Cor 10:4). We communicate a change in thinking so that eventually listeners will change their behaviors. But in order for any of that to happen, you have to help them follow your train of thought.

If they're going to laugh with the punch line, the audience must be with you every step of the way getting there. When introducing a new idea, one your audience has not heard before, you've got to create a path for them to approach it. The same is true when it comes to having people apply a message: you've got to walk them through the process of application; you must make a case and help them see it.

The most reliable way to help people follow your train of thought is to start by reviewing previous material or give away the end from the beginning. Go slow during the transitions, repeat your major points often, and every chance you get, connect the dots.

When the churchpeople listened to Jesus' preaching, they understood his train of thought; he let them see where he was going. He didn't say it, but he let them see it. They didn't like it, but they saw it.

Be clear about your own thought process. You should be able to summarize it very simply. If you don't know it, there is no way your audience will be able to get on board.

56

KEEP YOUR
POLITICS TO YOURSELF

Welcome anyone who is weak in faith, but not
for disputes over opinions.

—Romans 14:1

We know this axiom may be controversial. Ironically, our goal with it is to keep your parish from unnecessary controversy.

Neither of us is apolitical. Both of us, in fact, are interested in and closely follow politics. Nor do we believe that the Church should stay out of politics altogether. The Church certainly needs to have a clear voice in the temporal realm, and the bishops certainly need to play an incredibly important, in fact prophetic, role in our society. When it comes to issues of the right to life, religious freedom, civil rights, poverty, and immigration, the Church must speak out; we dare not be silent.

But when it comes to *your* preaching and teaching in *your* parish, keep *your* political views to *yourself.*

Look at scripture. Jesus resisted every effort to allow his kingdom movement to become a political movement. When the crowds wanted to make him king, he retreated to a quiet place. When asked about taxes, he simply said, pay them: give to God what is God's, and give to Caesar what is Caesar's.

Paul likewise said very little about the politics of the day. The consistent advice he gives to Christians is to obey the political leaders and to fulfill their responsibilities; otherwise, he never addresses political issues of the day, many of which were at odds with Christianity.

Why? It all comes down to influence. What influence do we want to have over people's lives? Do we want to change their vote or change their lives? Do we want to change their habits or their hearts?

We have only a few minutes each week at best to communicate. That's it, and that represents a small but distinct window of opportunity to be strategic in our message. Do we want to influence people politically or do we want to influence people with the message of the Gospel and then encourage them to make the application to all areas of their lives, including their politics?

Paul understood well that the Christians in Rome were in a very difficult position, politically speaking. When it came to discipleship and evangelization, he taught that the most effective strategy didn't involve debates but rather hospitality. The same holds true for our preaching and teaching. Don't try to trip people up or prove them wrong. Don't fight with them. Welcome them.

57

ASK YOURSELF
THE RIGHT QUESTIONS

The king went up to the house of the LORD with all the people of Judah and the inhabitants of Jerusalem: priests, Levites, and all the people, great and small. He read aloud to them all the words of the book of the covenant that had been found in the house of the LORD. . . . He thereby committed all who were in Jerusalem . . . to the covenant of God.

—2 CHRONICLES 34:30, 32

The purpose of all our communication is to lead to life change: getting the unchurched on the discipleship path and helping disciples go deeper. We *inform* in order to transform. (See pages 197–198.) The information we're sharing is important; it matters because it leads to the transformation of our character and conduct. Ask yourself three questions to keep focused on presenting information that leads to transformation.

What Do You Want Them to Know? What is the basic point you're trying to communicate?

Sometimes you might be presenting new information that your audience hasn't heard before. In fact, in our increasingly post-Christian society, more and more of what we have to say is news to many people. On the other hand, sometimes what you want people to know is something they have already been exposed to; they don't have to be taught so much as reminded. Either way, do you know what that is? We call this the *sermon in a sentence.* If you can't reduce your message to a single sentence, do you really know what you want your audience to know?

Why Do You Want Them to Know It? This is a question that is often left unaddressed, especially in churchworld. We just go out there and tell people stuff. *Why? Because we say so, that's why.* This might be breaking news in churchworld, but that approach no longer works. We need to know and effectively communicate why what we're communicating matters and deserves our audience's attention.

What Do You Want Them to Do, and Why Do You Want Them to Do It? This is about application and motivation: painting a picture of an action step that can positively impact and change the listener, helping him or her grow as a disciple of Jesus Christ.

The last successful and faithful king of Judah was Josiah. Chronicles tells us that he did what was right in the eyes of the Lord. He did more than that, too. He stepped up to his leadership role and, through effective communication, helped his people do what was right before the Lord as well. The results were life changing for the people and transformative for the nation. That's the kind of communication we should be working toward.

58

MASTER THE ART OF SUBTLETY

He then addressed this parable to those who were convinced of their own righteousness and despised everyone else. "Two people went up to the temple area to pray; one was a Pharisee and the other was a tax collector."

—LUKE 18:9–10

We have found that the most successful church leaders are clearly and consistently reminding members about the fundamental steps they should be taking as growing disciples. In turn, successful leaders look for opportunities in everything they communicate to reinforce those basic behaviors. The challenge is that repeatedly asking something can easily become needless nagging—unless you learn to employ subtlety.

Subtlety, though not simply defined or easily recognized, is all about delicacy and refinement. When we are asking people to do something we want them to do but they do not necessarily want to do—such as take a step in discipleship—*and* we intend to keep asking them until they do it, well, a certain subtlety serves us well.

TRY THESE TOOLS

USE SUBTLETY IN LITANIES AND LISTS

Tom: Drop subtle suggestions into your litanies and lists of examples. For example, not long ago we were actively recruiting for some additional staff positions. The openings were posted on our website and Facebook; they were included in the announcements at weekend Masses. But one Sunday, we slipped them into the weekend message, too. Michael was talking about God's vision for people's lives, and he said, "Maybe God wants to heal your marriage or revive your business. Maybe God is calling you to work for this church."

USE SUBTLETY IN NAMING HEROES

If you want people serving in ministry in your church, name and publically thank those who are already doing it. What gets rewarded with such public recognition will be replicated by others. You are teaching your congregation to emulate them.

USE SUBTLETY IN REAL-LIFE ILLUSTRATIONS AND CASUAL ASIDES

Another way you can subtly communicate steps you want people to take is by using illustrations from your own life. If you want people in your church to get in a small group, look for opportunities to talk about your own group. Just mentioning you are in a group is a gentle reminder to your church members that you want them in a group.

In his own communication, Jesus understood both the importance of subtlety and the value of being intentional about the use of examples. They might seem in opposition or even mutually exclusive. The fact is they serve each other well and make your communication more effective.

59

USE NOTES SLYLY

Rolling up the scroll, he handed it back to the attendant and sat down ... "Today this scripture passage is fulfilled in your hearing."

—LUKE 4:20, 21

Father Michael: I suppose I'm more of a writer than a speaker. Add to that a healthy strain of perfectionism and you'll usually find me obsessing over the text when it comes to homilies and presentations. Notes were a crutch for me. I didn't just rely on them; I was reading them. Reading to an audience is a form of communication for sure, but it's not as immediate or relational as speaking to them.

Tom: Notes, outlines, and even complete texts are all fine; it is a question of knowing how you hold and remember information, how you think on your feet, and basically what works for you. When I am speaking, I use an outline, but the body of the talk, the text, is all in my head. The outline helps me find or hold my place.

Father Michael: I still use a complete text when speaking; I just don't read it anymore. I have my own quirky system of color coding words and phrases, memorizing not the text itself but the look, what I call the "landscape," of the page. It is now easy for me to walk away from the podium and deliver a phrase or paragraph, even though

I have no idea what comes next, because I know exactly where I am in the text.

If I am away from the podium and lose my place, I simply repeat the phrase I am on as I return to my notes and find what's next. If I am distracted, and forget even what it is I am talking about (which happens all the time), I simply stop, return to my notes, pick them up deliberately, and say, "I have here in my notes. . . ."

Don't be afraid to use your notes in ways that work for you; just don't read them. And (this is important) don't ever refer to them when you are asking people to do something or issuing a challenge. Make sure you are looking your audience in the eyes when you do that.

Jesus delivers his first sermon in his hometown synagogue at Nazareth. As described in Luke's gospel, he evidently knew exactly what reaction he would get, and he got it. Be similarly deliberate about your communication style, including your use of notes.

Don't use notes as a crutch or an excuse for proper preparation, but definitely don't be shy about using them to your advantage and to make your task lighter and less labor intensive. Just use them slyly.

60

TELL STORIES

With many such parables he spoke the word to them as they were able to understand it. Without parables he did not speak to them.

—Mark 4:33–34

Tom: When I put my kids to bed at night, they always want a story. The skeptic in me assumes they're just trying to delay bedtime (which, by the way, they are). But I can also easily remember from my own childhood how stories caught my attention and captivated my imagination, as well as imparting important life lessons:

David and Goliath: When God is with us, we can stand up to giants.

The Tortoise and the Hare: Slow and steady wins the race.

The Little Engine That Could: Persevere through times of trouble.

As kids we clamor for stories, and they form a vital part of our development. You probably have stories you remember from childhood that you loved and loved to hear over and over again.

Scripture is full of stories. Jesus told them all the time because he knew the power they have to win and hold an audience's attention. He understood how much more effective a story could be when it came to answering a question or making a point.

- When asked who was his neighbor, he told the story of the Good Samaritan.

- When the Pharisees criticized him for eating with tax collectors and sinners, he told the story of the prodigal son.
- When asked by Peter about mercy and forgiveness, he told the story of the unmerciful servant.

Stories are not passive; they actively engage us. Stories are part entertainment, part instruction. They can inspire us, too; they can introduce us to different patterns and new behaviors.

TRY THESE TOOLS

TELL THE STORIES OF THE HEROES OF THE BIBLE AND THE SAINTS OF THE CHURCH

The lives of the saints and the great figures in the Bible can all begin to sound like fairy tales or at least examples of behaviors so far beyond our reach as to be nearly unhelpful. They are not, and we need to tell their stories in ways that make them real.

TELL YOUR STORY

Canned stories have a groan factor. They feel fake and inauthentic to your audience (because they are). Real stories that really happened to you can have an incredible impact. Most everyone will be interested in them.

TELL OTHER PEOPLE'S STORIES

Save e-mails and letters that you receive when people share their stories with you, especially how your church had an impact on their lives.

Keep a running file of the stories that come your way. Interview people or catch their testimony on video, and use it in your teaching and preaching.

There are few things more interesting or appealing to us and our human nature than storytellers and their storytelling, which is why Jesus relied on them. We love stories because we're all part of an awesome one—the story of creation and redemption. And that's the story we're telling over and over again, in many and varied ways.

61

TIMING IS EVERYTHING

There is an appointed time for everything, and
a time for every affair under the heavens.
—ECCLESIASTES 3:1

Father Michael: In 1994, I was serving as secretary to
Cardinal William Keeler, Archbishop of Baltimore. We
were very excited when it was announced that Pope
John Paul II was coming to our city. Then, quite unfortunately for him and us, the pope slipped and fell, seriously injuring himself. The trip was cancelled. We were
sad for his injury and deeply disappointed at the lost
opportunity. But the cancellation, which turned out to
be only a postponement, was the best thing that could
have happened. The extra year gave us additional time
as well as the huge advantage of better understanding
the project at hand.

Tom: At the end of 2012, we had plans to launch a capital
campaign to build a new church. Then, just as we were
preparing to get started, a significant piece of property
in our neighborhood became available. We immediately knew this new opportunity had to be explored even
though it meant the campaign would be delayed for
another year. While we felt anxious and annoyed by the
delay, it was the best thing that could have happened:
when we finally got around to that campaign, the econo-
my was more robust, the parish was more prepared, and
the campaign was a complete success.

Timing is critically important when it comes to launching any kind of program or project, and it is even more important in communications.

Always carefully consider your timing when it comes to preparing your preaching and teaching. We didn't launch our capital campaign in summer because people in our parish are on vacation. For the same reason, it is the wrong time to try recruiting volunteers. Be aware of the liturgical season as well as the season of your community's culture. Your communication needs to match your community.

Here in Timonium, September is a time of fresh starts when families are all about back-to-school matters. October and November are great times to get involved and it's usually when we see more volunteerism. December is about getting ready for Christmas. In January, everyone is setting New Year's resolutions and new behaviors; consequently, it's a great time to talk about small groups. February and March are the most popular times of the year to come to church because Lent still has a resonance, even for cultural Catholics. After Mother's Day, attendance dips, people are preoccupied, and we're back in the summer mode, so we know we need a lighter touch when it comes to communication.

Timing is also about pacing: sober and serious have their place, but they must be balanced by light and fun. The series after our capital campaign brought a lighter, simpler message, which essentially gave people a break. We had pushed hard for five weeks, and so another intense series would have been poor timing and probably not well received.

Timing matters when it comes to the presentation itself. Humor requires timing. Well-placed silence and effectively holding the silence requires timing, too.

The beautiful teaching of the book of Ecclesiastes offers wise counsel concerning our experience of time. As it turns out, there *is* a time for everything. Good communication understands and reflects that.

62

PREACHING ISN'T EASY

〈────────〉

Proclaim the word; be persistent whether it is convenient or inconvenient; convince, reprimand, encourage through all patience and teaching.

—2 TIMOTHY 4:2

In his book *You Are the Message*, Roger Ailes, the political strategist, tells the story of meeting President Ronald Reagan during his 1984 campaign for reelection. Reagan was called "The Great Communicator" and his communication skills were widely recognized as his greatest asset as a candidate. And yet, Ailes was recruited because the president was not doing well. He was performing badly: doubting himself, second-guessing his strategy, communicating poorly, and constantly coming across as confused and unprepared. If you know your history, Reagan robustly recovered from his slump, won the second debate, and went on to win the election in a landslide.

What turned things around for him in that campaign was hard work and positive encouragement. Ailes drilled the president daily, gave him honest feedback on what wasn't working, and praised him lavishly for what did.

Week in and week out, the work of preaching and teaching is never going to be easy. However good we get at it, whatever accolades we win, and however many fans we have, it is never going to be easy. And then, sometimes, things will not go well; we're suddenly stumbling, and what wasn't easy becomes incredibly difficult. A commitment to stay with it and the help of positive reinforcement are indispensable.

Preaching and teaching are essential, *and* they're difficult to do. That is why you have to love what you do enough to keep at it. No matter what life and the demands of the world bring, as Paul counsels Timothy, be persistent. That's one secret to success in a single sentence. Be persistent.

63

PREACHING IS A CRAFT

Do you see those skilled at their work? They will stand in the presence of kings.

—Proverbs 22:29

Tom: My family has visited Mount Vernon, George Washington's Virginia estate, on several occasions. It is a very cool place. The house and grounds are beautiful; there is a great museum and a working farm. A lot of care and attention have clearly been taken to make visitors feel as if they are stepping back into history. Every time we go there, my son Gus asks to visit the blacksmith shop, where he will sit endlessly transfixed while the blacksmith plies his craft. He heats up the furnace, casts the metal into the fire, forges it into shape, draws the metal to the desired dimension, and then brushes it to a finish. Seeing a blacksmith work his craft is fascinating. If you're watching a master craftsman, it's riveting.

Like blacksmithing, preaching is a craft. Craftsmanship requires both formulaic knowledge about how to do something—the ability to actually do it—and dedication to constantly fine-tune that ability. Any genuine craft also requires an artist's touch that springs from a pure love of the work.

Proverbs teaches us to develop the skills we need now for the talent we already have. Take time to discern your gifts when it comes to communication, and determine the skills you need to develop to improve your craft. When you do, there are deep rewards.

64

PREACH TO YOUR WEAKNESSES

While Ezra prayed and acknowledged their guilt, weeping and prostrate before the house of God, a very large assembly of Israelites gathered about him, men, women, and children; and the people wept profusely.

—Ezra 10:1

If you are preaching the whole Gospel, you will certainly come across areas in which you live it in an exemplary way and, elsewhere, in ways in which you are perhaps far from the standards of Jesus Christ.

When preaching and teaching, the temptation is to ignore our failures, to hide them, or lie about them, dress them up as something else and pretend we are otherwise. We can just focus on what the Church says or what scripture teaches and not mention the fact that we don't live it ourselves. That's a mistake. Our weaknesses provide an excellent opportunity to be authentic with our audience and help them know they are not alone in their struggles. Speaking about our own struggles helps us grow, too.

To preach to your weaknesses, be sure you are growing in self-awareness; make it part of your daily quiet time. Then, whenever you are preparing a homily, use your preparation as an opportunity for personal growth. No matter what topic you are addressing, even if you consider it a strength, you have an opportunity to grow. The first person who should apply your message is you.

The priest Ezra helps lead the way in Israel's restoration following the Exile. In that role, among other things, he has a big communication challenge before him. He longs to fulfill this role but is confronted with a serious gap in the faith of the people and their lived reality. Ezra turns to a very public, very authentic, and uncompromisingly honest prayer, which propels the people to begin to change everything.

We've heard others say it before: if you preach to your weaknesses, you'll never run out of things to say.

65

PREACH TO THE LOST

For the Son of Man has come to seek and to save what was lost.

—Luke 19:10

In traveling across the country to talk about *Rebuilt*, we have discovered a pervasive misconception about reaching those people Jesus calls "lost."

The lost are people—churched, unchurched, or dechurched—who do not have a loving relationship with the living Lord. Our discovery is that many churchpeople seem to believe that if you try to reach lost people then you are abandoning the work of growing disciples. We believe this is an insidious lie that is deeply destructive to evangelization efforts.

When Jesus called the first disciples to follow him, he didn't promise to make them stronger or smarter, bolder or brighter. He didn't even promise to make them holier. He only promised to make them "fishers of men." He connected the *following him* part to the *bringing other people into a relationship with him* part. Discipleship and evangelization go hand in hand. If we are truly following Jesus and growing in our discipleship, we are bringing people to him. Evangelization is a basic way in which we grow in discipleship. And discipleship leads to evangelization. But the point for our communication is that we begin with lost people because that's what the Lord told us to do.

Preaching to lost people helps churchpeople because it forces us to return again and again to the basics, which our churchpeople need as much as anyone else.

Preaching to lost people keeps us from sinking into theological language and churchy insider language that not just the lost, but a lot of churchpeople don't really understand. (See pages 136–137.)

Preaching to lost people helps churchpeople because you keep the focus on the struggles of the human condition that all of us, churched and unchurched, have. It strips away the pretense so many congregations operate under that we're an assembly of fully formed disciples.

On his final mission trip, Jesus visits Jericho. There, one more time, he returns to his basic approach to preaching and ministry and focuses on the lost: in this case, the very lost Zacchaeus. The churchpeople are astonished and appalled.

He does it anyway.

66

PREACH TO PEOPLE'S FELT NEEDS

Therefore I tell you, do not worry about your life, what you will eat [or drink], or about your body, what you will wear.

—MATTHEW 6:25

Recently, a tornado passed through our neighborhood, almost directly over our church. Warnings sounded on cell phones, and authorities issued stern instructions to take cover and stay away from windows. Since all of this is rare in our part of the world, it was an especially scary few minutes. But those announcements had our complete and undivided attention because they were communicating information we realized we needed to know.

A felt need is a concern that holds immediate relevance to people's lives. They know they need it; they feel it. People sit up and pay attention when they perceive what is being communicated could make a difference in their lives.

The problem with so much of our preaching and teaching is that it doesn't appear to be relevant to the lives of our listeners. Of course, such a view is profoundly ironic since what we are communicating is the lifesaving, life-changing message of Jesus Christ. But if it doesn't sound lifesaving or life changing, nobody is going to listen.

Churchpeople in churchworld like to talk about churchstuff. It's interesting to us. We love discussing *liturgy*, *ecclesiology*, *sacraments*, and oh yeah, *faith formation*. It's not that these things are unimportant or even that our congregations don't need to know and grow in their understanding and appreciation of their faith. We're just saying it's not the place to start. Start there and eyes glaze over and phones come out. Begin with what they care about, where their minds and hearts already are, and you'll have their attention. As you get to know your community, it becomes easier and easier. In our community, felt needs include money, marriage, marriage problems, raising kids, relationships, and emotional health.

For instance, we offered a Rite of Christian Initiation of Adults (RCIA) presentation on the Sacrament of Baptism. We taught that the baptized are anointed priest, prophet, and king. But we didn't start with that point, as people in our community don't have a lot of interaction with prophets and kings, and they think of priests as aloof figures with whom they have nothing in common. Instead, we started with the importance of living a life that is about servant leadership, truth telling, and sacrificial service. That got their attention.

We did a parents' prep for the Sacrament of Reconciliation. But we didn't start with an exhortation on regular use of confession because most people don't wan to hear that. We began with a discussion of the importance of helping kids learn to acknowledge when they are wrong and how making that a lifelong habit will build and strengthen their character. That got their attention.

Last Stewardship Sunday, we wanted to preach on, you guessed it, stewardship. But we didn't start from the perspective of "you need to give" or even "the parish needs your money." We started with a message about what the Bible says is the most effective way to handle your finances. That got their attention.

The towering teaching of Jesus that is called the Sermon on the Mount is, in effect, his inaugural message introducing the kingdom of God. But he didn't start there; he started with lots of practical advice about marriage, anger management, right relationships, and worry. That got their attention.

Part IV
ABOUT THE OUTCOMES

67

PREACH THE ANNOUNCEMENTS

/\\

The next day he saw Jesus coming toward him and said, "Behold, the Lamb of God, who takes away the sin of the world."

—John 1:29

Churches are in the communication business. That seems an excessively obvious, yet widely overlooked fact. We need to communicate the "Good News" of the kingdom of God. We need to communicate God's Word and how its application can change people's lives. We need to communicate the unparalleled value of the Eucharist as life-changing communion. We need to communicate the steps needed to make that application and get involved in that kingdom.

Churches are in the communication business and that's a tough business to be in. People have all kinds of information coming at them constantly and our parishioners are no different. Everything in the culture and everyone in the community is competing for their time and attention. To succeed, we've got to be disciplined and strategic about all our efforts.

Most parishes might have various instruments for communication—the bulletin, bulletin boards, announcements after Mass, posters in the lobby, the sign out front, and, of course, the parish website and the increasingly important parish app. However, these each pale in comparison to the pulpit.

We've found that when the pastor promotes an event or program from the pulpit, it takes on added weight—sometimes, in amazingly effective ways. In your parish, you can use that authority and power to communicate your announcements more successfully.

But don't waste the authority and power you have in your preaching on bake sale and bus trip announcements. We are *not* talking about those kinds of announcements. We're talking about the really important one. The one that will change your parish: the announcement of the kingdom of God and the invitation to become disciples. We're talking about announcing what that looks like in people's lives, the habits they need to form in their discipleship.

Preach the need for daily quiet time, weekly worship at Mass, the necessity of ministry and missions, the value of giving and tithing, small groups, increased use of the Sacrament of Penance. Preach *those* announcements.

And don't try to tackle the whole of discipleship every weekend. From time to time, devote the entire weekend message to a single discipleship habit: ministry, missions, small groups, giving/tithing, *or* confession. We'll even be upfront about it saying, for instance, "The purpose of this message is to convince you to volunteer in ministry."

On the other hand, you can be peppering your message with encouragement in their discipleship. So, if we're talking relationships, we might say (in an off-handed way), "Your need for relationships, by the way, is why we encourage small groups." If we're talking about sin, we might say, "Confessions are next Saturday from 1 to 3 p.m."

In other words, preach steps, *announce* steps. Give them specific steps to take that will cultivate healthy habits. If you're talking about daily quiet time, point them to resources they can use to help make it happen. If you're talking about small groups, give them an opportunity to sign up and get involved. If you're talking about getting into mission or ministry service, tell them how to do it, in a way that's easy and accessible.

The biggest announcement of all, the biggest announcement that ever came was in John the Baptist's recognition of the coming of the Christ. It is a remarkable and striking moment in the history of Revelation, which, if you think about it, is a history of announcements. Over and over again in scripture, from Genesis to Acts, God announces what he's going to do and what he wants us to do, too. That announcement, in all of the particular ways it is announced in our parishes, is foundational to our message.

68

ONE CHURCH, ONE MESSAGE

So that they may all be one, as you, Father, are in me and I in you, that they also may be in us, that the world may believe that you sent me.

—JOHN 17:21

Each week at Mass, we recite the Creed. When we do, we're acknowledging our belief in *one* Church. The Church is one, and our unity is given expression in everything from our liturgical calendar to the *Catechism*. Serving one another, caring for one another, and loving one another are all ways in which give expression to this unity. We are most perfectly one in the Eucharist.

Perhaps the clearest way to model and advance deep recognition and outward expression of unity (communion) in your parish is to work toward unity when it comes to all your parish communication. We like to say, one church, one message.

Why this concept, widely and successfully used in evangelical churches, hasn't yet caught on in the Catholic community is puzzling, since it can be so powerful and helpful. Its absence, on the other hand, can be divisive, even deeply debilitating. Imagine a football team that didn't call plays. The team would be all over the field. Think of the cast of a play each working with a different script or a meeting where each person refers to a different agenda.

The Church is a movement. That means we've got to move. And if we're actually ever going to get anywhere, we've got to move in the same direction, toward the same destination—discipleship in Christ.

One church, one message is simply about getting everybody in your parish headed in the same direction, as with geese flying in formation, or a crew rowing together.

TRY THESE TOOLS

YOUR PULPIT

The pulpit is the rudder of the parish. Wherever the preaching goes on a consistent basis, the church will move in that direction. We contend that the disparity in weekend homilies, from Mass to Mass and week to week, is the single biggest reason parishes struggle to be effective when it comes to evangelization and discipleship. When there are different or even conflicting messages, the people in our pews don't know where to go or what to do, so they don't go anywhere; they don't do anything. If the preaching is scattered or unclear, the parish will be without direction. To be a movement, every member of the parish needs to hear the same or at least a similar message. It is their opportunity to receive spiritual direction for the week ahead and move in the direction you set. Do whatever it takes so that all the people who come to Mass hear the same message. If there are multiple celebrants in your parish on weekends, at the very least they can be meeting and coordinating consistent themes and challenges. Better yet, they could take turns, one preacher preaching all the Masses on a given weekend and someone else the following week, etc. (This would also mean less work for your clergy.)

YOUR PROGRAMS

Our children's and student programs, as well as our adult small groups, follow the same topic in their weekly curriculum that is addressed in the weekend homily. In this way, we are continuing to shape the conversation of our whole parish. For instance, if we are doing a message on persevering in prayer, forgiving your enemy, or living in hope, everybody hears it at Mass, kids learn about it in kids' programs, and small groups discuss it when they gather later in the week. (See pages 128–129.)

YOUR PRINTED AND ELECTRONIC COMMUNICATION: ONE MESSAGE

Website, bulletin, social media, or whatever communication you use should be a reflection of your one message.

In his final prayer at the Last Supper, Jesus prayed that his Church would be united, that we would be one. There he gave us the Eucharist that this might literally and eternally be so. That's because the unity of the Church is meant to be a reflection of the unity of the Trinity and God's love for the world. The unity of your parish begins in Christ; it grows in grace. Your coherent, unified communication serves that growth.

69

JUST START
A CONVERSATION

Do not conform yourselves to this age but be
transformed by the renewal of your mind.

—Romans 12:2

In our spiritual lives, change and growth largely depend on our *thinking*. What we think about God will ultimately determine our relationship with him. Is he a cosmic cop and a religious rule giver? Perhaps he's just an absence where there was supposed to be a presence, an old-fashioned, outdated idea, or mostly a myth. Or is God really a loving Father and the living Lord?

Effective evangelization and discipleship often come down to overcoming our postmodern skepticism and changing our thoughts. It's simply learning to think about God as he reveals himself to us and then coming to see the world and one another as he teaches us to see. Our thinking will then determine our behavior. The habits of Christian life are the products of our right thinking. Serving, giving, daily prayer, forgiving those who hurt us, and loving our enemies are all fruits of a change in thinking.

In our parishes, we are engaged in a battle for people's minds and hearts. If we win there, we have a shot at changing behaviors, which leads to changed lives. So, the more we can get people *thinking*, the more effective we're going to be.

It begins, simply enough, by talking about it. That's why we like to say that we're just trying to get a conversation started. Maybe it starts at church, but it doesn't end there. We want the conversation to continue everywhere in our community. The more our members are talking about our message, the more they are potentially growing as disciples. And the more they bring others into the conversation, the more they are evangelizing.

TRY THESE TOOLS

BE CONSISTENT

Here it is again: one church, one message. (See pages 163–165.) The more everyone is hearing the same thing and sharing a common point of reference, the wiser the conversation is likely to become. A parishioner tells the story of being at his neighborhood pool one summer Sunday afternoon. Another parishioner greeted him and began discussing that day's homily. Immediately others joined in, too. They could do that because, even though they had all gone to different Masses, they had all heard the same message.

BE RELEVANT

Speak on relevant topics people care about, and answer questions people are actually asking. (See pages 158–159.) We heard a story from a mom with older children, driving home from church one Sunday and actually getting into a heated conversation about what had been discussed at church that day. We apologized for creating the conflict, but the mom was delighted: instead of just fighting with each other, they were fighting about ideas that actually mattered to them.

BE A CHURCH OF SMALL GROUPS

Small groups are faith-sharing circles that meet for support, prayer, accountability, and discipleship. And they are destinations for the conversations we're talking about. Start a small-group program in your parish, and encourage your parishioners to get into a group. One of our new members recently told us the story of being invited to a guys' group, even though he was not then going to church. He went mostly to air his grievances with God, the Catholic Church in particular, and organized religion in general. It was this small group that heard him out and eventually changed his mind.

St. Paul teaches the Romans a lesson we need to be reminded of from time to time: disciples are called to a certain detachment from the world and a willingness to engage in the realm of higher realities. All of our communication efforts should aim at helping parishioners with the transformation of their thinking. And that actually starts happening simply enough in the conversations you start.

70

CREATE TENSION

The Philistines were stationed on one hill and the Israelites on an opposite hill, with a valley between them. . . . The Philistine continued: "I defy the ranks of Israel today. Give me a man and let us fight together." When Saul and all Israel heard this challenge of the Philistine, they were stunned and terrified.

—1 Samuel 17:3, 10–11

Tension is the pressure between two proximate but distinct things, whatever they may be: borders, boundaries, positions, views, personalities, or feelings. We often think of them as bad, but we actually need stress and tension. In fact, we seek it out; that's why we love competitive sports and cliff-hanging drama. It's why people are attracted to daredevil adventures and flock to thrill-seeking adventure. It is why we work out: we increase the stress on our body, to strengthen our heart and build muscle. We increase our stress and tension because it can be exciting, awaking us to life and forcing us to grow! Stress and tension take us to new levels we could not get to without them.

When you identify the spiritual and emotional tension people experience, but never name, when you share the fears and worries that keep people up at night even though they would never disclose them to their closest friends, you are creating tension. And it is actually a powerful tension that effectively opens them up to life change.

In the battle between Israel and the Philistines, God allows the tension to run high and at length. He waits forty days before providing a resolution, and even when he does, it doesn't sound like a plan; it sounds like an absurd mistake: a boy steps forward to face a giant. Talk about great tension.

The Bible answers the deepest questions of the human heart and every possible experience of life. It doesn't just give us the answers; it helps us form the questions themselves. The questions, together with the answers, provide an essential tension to the whole.

God creates tension in our lives so that we are desperately crying out for him to act, so that we can more clearly see his power at work, and so that we can come at last to see him as our Savior.

71

SILENCE CREATES TENSION

Upon learning that he was under Herod's juris-
diction, Pilate sent him to Herod who was in Jerusalem at that time. . . . Herod questioned him
at great length, but he gave him no answer.

—Luke 23:7, 9

The Jews answered, "We have a law, and according to that law he ought to die, because he
made himself the Son of God." Now when Pilate
heard this statement, he became even more
afraid, and went back into the praetorium and
said to Jesus, "Where are you from?" Jesus did
not answer him. So Pilate said to him, "Do you
not speak to me?"

—John 19:7–10

The "power pause" is a technique described by author James C. Humes. He argues that before you speak, you should try to lock eyes with your listeners, all of them or some of them depending on the size of the group. Stand and stare; demand and command their attention. They *will* listen. A deliberate pause before you speak communicates poise and confidence, even power and purpose.

We like to expand his instruction. Silence, both at the beginning of a message and at well-timed intervals throughout, creates a tension that increases attention because it raises curiosity about what will be said next.

Silence is unfamiliar, even uncomfortable, in our noisy world. And sometimes in our messages we want to make our audience a little uncomfortable; we want to throw them off balance just enough so that they will take the journey with us to figure out how to restore it.

You can also use silence for dramatic effect or to make a point. Use silence to punctuate a point you have just made, or after a memorable line to underscore it. The silence allows the point to sink in; it forces your audience to ponder the point and turn it over in their minds. Many memorable lines are missed because they get lost in all the words that follow.

> **Father Michael:** Silence is a way to simply start a new section of your message, too. It's one of my favorite techniques, and I use it all the time. I'll finish a section of my message, stop, rearrange my papers, perhaps take a sip of water, and then after some deliberate silence begin a new section. The change of topic forces listeners to unconsciously be thinking about how the new point or new material connects with what I had been talking about earlier. It can almost serve as a refresh button.

In the powerful and emotionally charged sequence of the Passion narrative, there are two moments of stunning silence: Jesus before Herod and Jesus before Pilate. Why doesn't he speak? Both are opportunities to save himself before authorities who have the power and disposition to do exactly that. And yet he steadfastly refuses to do so. Jesus remains silent, and the tension leaps off the pages of scripture.

Silence is an important tool in your preaching. Make sure that you use it.

72

HOLD OFF ON ANSWERS

O stupid Galatians! Who has bewitched you, before whose eyes Jesus Christ was publicly portrayed as crucified? I want to learn only this from you: did you receive the Spirit from works of the law, or from faith in what you heard? Are you so stupid? After beginning with the Spirit, are you now ending with the flesh?

—GALATIANS 3:1–3

As Catholic Christians, we steward and serve the Word of God. With two thousand years of tradition, scripture, magisterial teaching, and shared experience living in and learning from that Word, we have world-changing wisdom to pass on. Our job as communicators is to awaken people's curiosity for this information, especially the people who might be coming back to our churches for the first time in a long time, or the first time ever. Sadly, in our own day, there is a distinct lack of interest in our deposit of faith, so the challenge is a daunting one.

As we argued in a previous axiom (see pages 169–170), a great way to awaken interest is to create tension. This axiom argues that a great way to create tension is to ask tough questions. And here's the key to tough questions: hold off on answers as long as possible.

If we give away the answer before the question is raised or before people are fully engaged in the question then they will have no lasting interest in our message.

Build tension by raising tough questions:

- If God is good and all powerful, then why is there pain?
- Why does evil seem so attractive?

• Why do bad things happen to good people?

Work to get people thinking, "Yes, I want to know the answer to that question. I want to know why that is so." Then promise that you are going to examine the question and that scripture helps provide an answer. Asking questions in a message, at the right time, helps people put their own skin in the game, especially when they have to make a decision or judgment.

We see this kind of teaching in Jesus all the time. After taking the disciples to Caesarea Philippi, he didn't simply tell them that he was the Christ. Instead, Jesus asked the disciples, "Who do people say that I am?" After they answered, he asked another: "But who do *you* say that I am?" (Mk 8:27, 29). Jesus raised the level of tension and forced them to make a decision.

Jesus also used questions after he told stories so that his listeners were challenged to draw conclusions. When he was at the home of Simon the Pharisee, a "sinful" woman whom Simon would not accept socially came in to wash Jesus' feet with her tears. Jesus allowed her to do it, even though he knew it was making the Pharisees in the house extremely uncomfortable. He permitted the tension to mount; then he told a story of two people who owed a creditor money. One owed very much, and the other owed only a little. When they could not pay, the creditor forgave both debts. Then Jesus, in the midst of this great tension, increased the tension for Simon by asking, "Which of them will love [the creditor] more?" (Lk 7:42). Simon was forced to reply with the obvious answer: the one who owed more.

When the teacher of the law asked Jesus about the greatest commandment, Jesus told him to love God with all his heart, soul, mind, and strength. Then the teacher asked, "And who is my neighbor?" (Lk 10:29). Rather than just answering his question, Jesus told the story of the Good Samaritan who stopped to help a man beaten by robbers. Then Jesus increased the tension in the teacher when he asked yet another question: "And which of the three men was neighbor to the man who fell among robbers?" The teacher of the law was forced to deal with his own prejudice. Learning from Jesus draws people into our message and creates tension by asking questions right after a story.

Seemingly without any hesitation, St. Paul employs very pointed questions to the Christians in Galatia. Presumably he was creating quite a lot of tension. But he was obviously doing it for a purpose, which was always the single purpose he had in mind: advancing the Gospel of Jesus Christ.

73

SURPRISE ME

> David grew very angry with that man and said to Nathan: "As the Lord lives, the man who has done this deserves death! He shall make four-fold restitution for the lamb because he has done this and was unsparing." Then Nathan said to David: "You are the man!"
>
> —2 Samuel 12:5–7

Certain messages just seem to stick. They just do. Why?

In the book *Made to Stick*, authors Chip and Dan Heath argue that "sticky ideas"—ideas that have traction for audiences, ideas that people tend to grasp and hold on to, and ideas that take root in listeners—come from the unexpected. In other words, they're a surprise. If you want to communicate with power, surprise your audience.

TRY THESE TOOLS

CHANGE DIRECTIONS

You can grab people's attention when you pursue an argument in a certain course and then change course and go in another or even the opposite direction. Care must be taken that this isn't confusing to the listener, but when done well it is a most effective communication tool.

CHANGE PATTERNS

As with a change in direction, you can establish a pattern and then discard it and go with a new pattern. The sudden change will catch your audience's attention.

USE PROPS

Not all the time, not every time, but sometimes, or from time to time, use props.

> **Father Michael:** In a message series all about what we were calling "counterfeit gods," I shared an observation I made while watching a football game. A player, after scoring a touchdown, triumphantly carried the football around the perimeter of the field as the crowd rose, raised their hands, and roared in jubilation. My point was that the whole display was idolatry, and the crowd was involved in idol worship. Anyway, to everyone's surprise I pulled a football out of the pulpit, held it up, and repeated in a plaintive kind of way, "It's just a football. It's just a football." People still talk about it. I am *very* reluctant to use props: they can be a crutch, they can be a cliché, and they can be an excuse to avoid more solid communication. I do not use props more than once or twice a year, but when I do, they have added impact because they are unexpected and rare.

A very powerful message was preached by the prophet Nathan to the king, David. And all the story's devastating strength came in the surprise ending. Nathan's message more than got David's attention; it changed his heart and changed his life. Surprise in your communication can have that kind of power.

74

SHOCK ME

But the angel of the LORD called to him from heaven, "Abraham, Abraham!" "Here I am," he answered. "Do not lay your hand on the boy," said the angel. "Do not do the least thing to him. For now I know that you fear God, since you did not withhold from me your son, your only one."

—GENESIS 22:11–12

Surprise and shock are different. But both are important communication tools, so it is important to understand the difference. It's one of degrees. Surprise throws us off. It is the interruption of a pattern, something we just didn't expect in the normal course of things. Shock is not so much an interruption as it is a termination, an abrupt end to our previous understanding of how the world works or individuals operate. Surprise catches our attention. Shock disturbs us to our core.

Do we really want to shock people? Yes, sometimes.

What is shocking probably introduces us to new behaviors or changed attitudes. Think about it: when you've heard shocking information about someone, your attitude toward them changes. If you discover something shocking about your family, you might rethink your house rules. If you receive shocking news about your health, you will probably change your lifestyle. Shock does not bring a positive connotation, but it need not always be negative.

Jesus shocked his audiences all the time. For example, one time he said, "Unless your righteousness surpasses that of the scribes and Pharisees, you will not enter into the kingdom of heaven" (Mt 5:20). The scribes and Pharisees were considered the most righteous people in the culture. They were the professional churchpeople who devoted all their time to being righteous. There was no way the audience listening to Jesus' message that day could surpass that kind of righteousness. Jesus completely threw his audience off; he utterly dismissed their established view of thought. And then he proceeded to tell them how to surpass the righteousness of the scribes and the Pharisees.

Another time, Jesus stood in front of a dead man's tomb and said, "Lazarus, come out!" (Jn 11:43). And the dead man walked out. Now, that's shocking, and it got so much attention it set in motion the events leading to Jesus' murder.

Perhaps most shocking of all, or ever, Jesus said to his friends and followers, "Unless you eat the flesh of the Son of Man and drink his blood, you do not have life within you" (Jn 6:53). Why did Jesus challenge them in such a shocking way? Well, the crowds wanted to make him king, and they totally misunderstood the type of kingdom he was building, the kind of king he would be. And so at an appropriate time, he shocked them with this truth. As a result, many of his disciples left him.

We need to shock people at times to move them out of their complacency, to correct a huge error in thinking, or sometimes even to prune our churches.

> **Father Michael:** The most unforgettable example of this in our experience came a few years ago. We usually say that rebuilding our parish was a fifteen year process: five years to understand and acknowledge that we had a problem (our parish wasn't healthy or growing), five years to figure out at least the broad strokes of a way forward (reach the lost, make disciples), and then five years to implement that strategy.
>
> The final five brought a lot of conflict and tension: many people already in the pews were not interested in going where we were going and resisted at every opportunity. After a couple of years of guerrilla warfare, I recognized that we were getting nowhere; there were simply too many in the resistance. The balance needed

to change. So, one Sunday I gave a message that has become the stuff of legend around here.

I explained the Church is a movement not a monument, and as a parish, we were finally going to join that movement. And, *and* if you don't want to go you need to "get off the bus." Dozens did that very day; there were tears and cheers, outrage and euphoria, nearly a fist-fight in the parking lot, and lots of other reactions, too. Sure it was shocking, but if I had never given that message our parish would never have moved forward.

We can't try to shock people all the time; if we do, it will lose its value. But sometimes we need to. So put it in your toolbox for those occasions when you want to make a special impression.

Perhaps the only thing more shocking than God's revelation that Abraham would have a son was his command to sacrifice the boy. In turn, the reversal provided an even more shocking conclusion. Never underestimate the power of communication that is occasionally and strategically shocking.

75

COMFORT OUTSIDERS/ CHALLENGE INSIDERS

> They went away one by one, beginning with the elders. So he was left alone with the woman before him. Then Jesus straightened up and asked her, "Woman, where are they? Has no one condemned you?" She replied, "No one, sir." Then Jesus said, "Neither do I condemn you."
> —John 8:9–11

> Woe to you, scribes and Pharisees, you hypocrites.
> —Matthew 23:13

Imagine, you decide to dine at a restaurant for the first time. As your evening unfolds, you gradually discover things are not what you had expected. For starters, there's a dress code; jacket and tie are required. You have to eat your food in a certain order, with prescribed courses. The menu uses strange words and phrases to describe the food in a way that you largely don't understand. What you do order turns out to be not at all what you thought; it's unappetizing, even distasteful.

The maître d' is condescending, the waiter is slow, and the other guests unfriendly, in a way that makes you feel uncomfortable (as if they're somehow different than you). Worst of all, while making the rounds to flatter and fawn over the regulars, the chef inadvertently insults you; you can hear him making fun of people (like you) who don't appreciate his food. The regulars glare at your kids. Clearly there is nothing here for children. Finally, another couple shows up to tell you that you're actually sitting at *their* table. How soon would you go back there? How quickly would you find other things to do?

How much like that experience is the experience of your parish for the unchurched? Maybe more than a little.

So often our churches, and the message of our parishes, reflect that crazy restaurant. If new people do find their way to us, how we treat them, and especially what we say to them, is so often *not* helpful. Sometimes it can be worse than that, it can be insulting. It can turn guests off and send them away, sometimes for good.

On the other hand, we usually speak very differently, very carefully to insiders. We comfort the insiders, by saying exactly what they want to hear, what they expect to hear, what they've heard a thousand times before. We boldly affirm truths they already have and hold. And then we kind of let them off the hook with the ones they don't really care for.

Meanwhile we challenge outsiders to accept the world as we see it, and we comfort insiders with affirmation of the world as they want it. As a result, our congregations drift into complacency and often irrelevance. If you want to grow a healthy church community, you've got to turn that around.

Challenge insiders in the ways they need to hear, so that they can keep growing as disciples. We like to talk about this as "taking their next steps": giving (money and time), growing (in prayer), volunteering (in ministry). The basic challenge is to grow as a disciple, and when members are growing as disciples, guess what? It's more attractive to the unchurched.

Comfort outsiders by first of all speaking to them as if they're actually there, even if they're not (they never will be unless and until you start talking to them). Your basic message to them is "Relax, none of this applies to you." They always get a free pass when it comes to any kind of challenge beyond the challenge they've already met (showing up). And make sure you thank them for showing up, in front of the whole congregation.

Jesus was very clear about this in his preaching and teaching. The people he challenged most consistently were the churchpeople, the religious leaders of the day. With them he was often quite stern. On the other hand, he was nothing but loving to the lost. He just wanted to find them and help them get to know him better. Keep making that distinction as you rebuild your message.

76

MAKE THEM LAUGH/MAKE THEM CRY

Then our mouths were filled with laughter; our
tongues sang for joy.... Those who sow in tears
will reap with cries of joy.

—PSALM 126:2, 5

We've already made the case that emotions are vital to communication. (See pages 125–127.) Two of the most powerful are laughter and tears. The movies we love and that do the best at the box office have us laughing one moment and crying the next.

Laughter and tears connect us to one another, and they provide healing for the heart and balm for the soul. We need the release of tensions and emotions that comes through tears and springs from laughter. If you make an audience laugh or cry (or both), you are connecting them to one another in community and bonding them more closely with the Church.

Obviously not every message needs to try to do everything. You should regularly rely on or look to laughter, though not each and every message requires it. You might not want to use it at a funeral (although it can be exceptionally helpful there, too). Make people cry less often. It's more of a special occasion tool.

So how do you do it?

You make people laugh by being funny. And the easiest, most reliable way to be funny is by making fun of yourself and being self-deprecating. Laughter also comes from the element of surprise and misdirection. You get your audience going one way and then go another. To get better at using humor in your message, pay attention to how you make others laugh in everyday conversations. Use the same type of humor in your presentations. Humor flows best out of our personalities, who we are.

We cry at pain, disappointment, and loss, especially the loss of time and life. We cry at the gap between where we are and where we want to be. Tears also come when we are humbled by great acts of service and generosity on the one hand or the admission of our own sins and shortcomings on the other. People cry when we call on their better angels. They cry when we point them to the highest of ideals or their greatest values.

Psalm 126 is a song of joy celebrating the great work of God, despite the sadness and sorrow of this world. That song should sing through all of our communication.

77

SAYING IT DOESN'T MAKE IT SO

Even so, on the outside you appear righteous, but inside you are filled with hypocrisy and evildoing.

—Matthew 23:27, 28

Father Michael: While visiting a community in another part of the country (nope, I won't say where), I happened to be staying across the street from a Catholic church. This particular church had hung handsome banners on its facade proclaiming, "All are welcome." One Saturday afternoon, I noticed the front doors were open, evidently for Mass. I decided to check it out. Once inside the narthex, a group of guys, whose nameplates identified them as ushers, stopped cold in their conversation and stared at me as I passed through. In the otherwise empty church, a group of women (the ushers' wives?) were kneeling in the pews near the altar, praying the Rosary. I decided to join them. As I took my place in a nearby pew, one by one each of the women turned and glared at me. A glare is more intense than a stare by the way, and that's what it felt like they did to me: without missing a single beat when it came to their recitation of the Rosary, they glared at me. I felt like an unwanted outsider, so I left.

It is easy to understand the instinct to say something is so when we want it to be so, hoping that saying it will make it so. We say "good job" to a struggling beginner or "we're so glad you came" to an unexpected visitor. Perhaps it's helpful; it's certainly harmless. But if the gap grows too wide between what is said and what is so, we can drift into insincerity or even hypocrisy. And for some reason this is always a particularly persistent problem in churchworld.

Saying it simply doesn't make it so.

If we say we are here to serve the poor but we never actually lift a finger to help the impoverished in our community, or worse, turn them away if they happened to show up at our door, well, that's a problem.

If we say we want to raise more mature givers and consistently teach the biblical principle of the tithe, but we keep nickel and diming people to death with fundraisers, well, there's a problem.

If we advertise that all are welcome and then glare at a newcomer, well, that's a problem, too.

Jesus reserved his harshest criticism for the hypocrisy of the religious establishment of his time. They simply didn't live what they preached. We must be vigilant that there is close alignment between our words and our action. Our communication should always be a completely accurate expression of who we are striving to be.

78

TO BE DYNAMIC, YOU'VE GOT TO BE SPECIFIC

> Then he took the bread, said the blessing, broke it, and gave it to them, saying, "This is my body, which will be given for you."
>
> —Luke 22:19

When it comes to the task of communication on behalf of the kingdom of God, we are trying to give expression to realities such as grace, beauty, and truth. That is no simple task since they're somewhat, if not largely, intangible.

On the other hand, it's easier to just keep everything abstract. And sometimes churchpeople like it better that way, too; abstractions give us lots of wiggle room, truth can come to be whatever we want it to be, beauty is in the eye of the beholder, and grace is about feeling good. Anything can mean whatever you want it to mean, and application can be made in ways that are convenient and comfortable.

Besides, getting specific and making our message concrete can sound as if we're oversimplifying things. That is actually a comment we hear from critics all the time: "You're just dumbing it down." But, we would argue, getting concrete and specific is not dumbing it down; it's drilling down to where a message can have a real impact. Good communication is specific. What makes it specific? You can imagine it with your senses; you know it from your experience; and you've seen it with your own eyes.

When we're vague, we're not really helping our parishioners grow as disciples; we're probably giving them a free pass instead. And when it comes to the unchurched, our vagueness is meaningless.

Don't allow yourself to get away with abstractions, especially when it comes to your examples. Pull them out of the lived experience of the community you are talking to. Be specific.

- Don't talk about sin; talk instead against dishing dirt about your neighbor's marriage with your best friend or at your kids' soccer game.
- Don't talk about giving to God; talk instead about signing up for automatic funds transfer, and where and how to do that.
- Don't just talk about prayer; talk about the specific eight minutes a day when they can pray, what they can say, and where they can say it.

A lot of Catholics don't really believe in spiritual realities because they've never been introduced to the specific implications of those realities. We have to make them specific:

- Charity toward our neighbor can change our hearts toward people we don't like.
- Giving to God can transform our finances.
- Prayer is a place where God will talk to us, answer our questions, and direct our daily living.

The mysterious, spooky night before he died, Jesus did something truly unexpected for his friends. He promised the gift of himself, in bread. Take it and eat it, and I'll be with you, is essentially his message. That's incomprehensible, but it is also immensely helpful.

Our Catholic faith is incredibly concrete and strikingly specific. The sacraments require specific *matter*. Wheat bread and grape wine are necessary to confect the Eucharist. Baptism demands water—no other liquid will do. Holy Orders, Confirmation, and Anointing of the Sick require certain kinds of oils. Penance and Marriage require specific words. The whole sacramental life of the Church is based on specifics. And this is as it should be since it is established on the most scandalously specific event in history—when the universal God became flesh in the person of Jesus of Nazareth.

79

AIM AT NOTHING AND YOU'LL HIT IT EVERY TIME

Just one thing: forgetting what lies behind but straining forward to what lies ahead, I continue my pursuit toward the goal, the prize of God's upward calling, in Christ Jesus.

—Philippians 3:13–14

A goal is the result or achievement toward which effort is directed; it's the aim or the end. In everything we do, we need a goal if we are going to succeed or even recognize success when we achieve it. Unfortunately, we do not always live with a full or lively awareness of our goals and thereby drift off toward the wrong ones.

When it comes to our church communication, we can easily end up with unintended outcomes and unhelpful goals.

- We have fifteen or twenty minutes to speak, and we just want to fill time.
- We just don't want to appear unprepared or stupid.
- We seek to win the approval and affirmation of our audience. We want to entertain and be funny.

Or worse still, we've lost sight of any particular goals, even the wrong ones. We're just talking because that's what we're paid to do and nobody is listening anyway, right? How many homilies have you heard, or how many classes have you sat through, where that seemed to be the attitude of the speaker?

Without the proper goals, our communication is not going to be the effective evangelization and discipleship tool it can be.

The Apostle Paul was always clear about his goal in preaching and teaching. And he was pretty successful.

Our goal is reaching the unchurched with the lifesaving message of Jesus Christ while equipping newcomers and parishioners alike to go deeper in their discipleship. Aim at that.

80

SHAPE ATTITUDES

/\

But we proclaim Christ crucified, a stumbling
block to Jews and foolishness to Gentiles.
—1 CORINTHIANS 1:23

Catholic biblical illiteracy is a sad fact, but it's not the parishioners' fault.
Blame belongs to parish priests and church leaders reaching back genera-
tions. The culprit is the whole Counter-Reformation culture that has prevailed in the Church for nearly five hundred years.

Before the introduction of the printing press, books were rare and expensive. People had to go to church to hear scripture. As books became
more readily available, Protestant reformers were encouraging the faithful
to read the Bible and, in many places, actually memorize it. Meanwhile,
Catholic leaders, fearing that personal scripture reading without the direction and authority of the Church could lead to serious error (and boy, oh
boy, did it), actually discouraged Bible reading. The Second Vatican Council clearly reversed this approach, encouraging biblical literacy under the
direction of the magisterium. But in the subsequent decades, little seems
to have changed; at least that's our perspective.

> **Father Michael:** Here's my take on why: it's our commu-
> nication of scripture. A lot of preaching and teaching im-
> plicitly teaches people to avoid scripture.

There was a preacher here at our parish who, instead of preaching, used
his time in the pulpit doing exegesis of the scripture texts. Every week, he
would work his way through the readings with his historical critical tools
and Greek and Hebrew translations. Week after week, he thereby proved,

beyond a shadow of a doubt, there was nothing in the text of interest to anyone but him.

Still another approach reduces the sum total of scripture to a single thing: perhaps a sledgehammer to frighten the guilty or a storybook to charm the innocent.

In addition, in many places and at this point for many years, Catholics have developed a skepticism toward the Word of God: it's not real; it has no practical application. In this approach, angels don't exist, and the Epiphany didn't really happen. Or there's this one: Jesus didn't actually multiply the loaves and fishes. What happened was that the people already had all the food that was needed; they were just hoarding it. When the little boy in the story shared his meal, Jesus motivated the others to do the same. In other words, the Word of God can't really be trusted.

> **Father Michael:** This was the theory asserted by the priest who taught scripture in my high school (that would be my Catholic high school). As a fearless sophomore, I challenged him in front of the whole class: "If Jesus could rise from the dead, he could multiply bread, so I guess you don't believe in the Resurrection either." I got detention for a whole week.

The quality of our preaching and teaching, as well as the content, will shape the way our parishioners approach and use scripture. One of our most important goals for communication, in youth and kids programs, small-group resources, and homilies, is to inspire in listeners a hunger to read scripture.

TRY THESE TOOLS

COMMUNICATE RESPECT FOR SCRIPTURE

Honor the Bible as the Word of God; allow this to be reflected in how you actually hold and handle it. Approach it with humility and reverence. But be authentic: if you struggle to understand a passage, let your audience know that.

COMMUNICATE THE ACCESSIBILITY OF SCRIPTURE

Let your listeners know that the Bible is filled with useful information. You can help people understand that they don't have to begin by believing everything in the Bible, they should just start using it and discover for themselves that it works.

COMMUNICATE ENTHUSIASM FOR SCRIPTURE

Help the people you're talking to see your attitude of enthusiasm, even excitement, shine through. That will be the natural fruit of the time you lovingly spend with it daily.

The Gospel of Christ is a miracle, which defied the wisdom and logic of the Roman world. The Jews were looking for a triumphant political leader, so it didn't make any sense to them either. St. Paul understood the attitudes of his audience, and he also understood his task as a communicator: to shape new attitudes toward scripture.

81

TAKE PEOPLE
ON A JOURNEY

For God said: If the people see that they have to fight, they might change their minds and return to Egypt. Instead, God rerouted them toward the Red Sea. . . . The LORD preceded them, in the daytime by means of a column of cloud to show them the way, and at night by means of a column of fire to give them light.

—Exodus 13:17–18, 21

As a church, we have the job of leading people into a growing relationship with Jesus Christ. This means that none of us is where we could be and should be in that relationship yet. It means that all of us have not only the need but also the ability to grow. We have potential for more. We can love God more. We can be kinder, more patient, and more accepting and loving of other people.

Spiritual leadership requires that we move people from where they are to where God wants them to be, and basically that's an exercise in communication. And to be most successful and achieve the widest possible effect, we will want to make it easy for them to move, especially when people are just coming back to church for the first time in a long time.

TRY THESE TOOLS

MEET THEM AND PICK THEM UP

It's first of all about reaching out to the people in front of you, meeting them wherever they are, spiritually, intellectually, culturally, and emotionally. Just as parents would pick up their kids and get them in the car, you must pick up your audience in your introduction. You do it by identifying and explaining *their* thoughts and feelings to them. Describe their experiences, name their struggles, and lay out their concerns and fears, their hopes and dreams. Rely on what is universal in the human experience. Establish questions that create tension and demand an answer. Any of these tools has the potential to pick people up and help them want to come with you.

TELL THEM WHAT GOD SAYS

Then you have to actually move people along by transitioning into what God says on a topic. Walk through a story or a passage of scripture that helps your listeners begin to see the topic through the lens of God's Word. The movement is from personal opinion and experience to God's Word and wisdom.

KNOW YOUR DESTINATION

Finally, taking people somewhere means we have a destination. There's got to be a "there" there. What do we want people to *do*? As a result of this journey, something about their lives needs to be *different* after the journey than it was before it. There needs to be an assignment or some simple homework and application to reinforce the point. It can be small; it doesn't have to be big, but it should be specific. Sometimes the assignment can be something you do as a crowd such as praying a prayer together, but you need to have a destination in mind.

God left nothing to chance when the Israelites took their great journey. He picked them up and took them where he wanted them to go, beginning with the spectacular parting of the Red Sea. But that wasn't all; he routed them around dangers and away from conflict, and gave them constant guidance and direction (not to mention their daily fare). Even so, and very much like many in our parishes, they were somewhat reluctant to even begin their journey and sometimes disposed to give it up entirely.

That's why he had to *take* them on the journey. Rebuild your message by getting good at doing that.

82

COMMUNICATE FOR LIFE CHANGE

Now, therefore, fear the LORD and serve him completely and sincerely. Cast out the gods your ancestors served beyond the River and in Egypt, and serve the LORD.

—JOSHUA 24:14

Why we do *what* we do matters. When we lose our *why*, we lose our *way*. We inevitably get lost when we don't know why we are doing what we are doing.

The purpose of the scriptures is to make us more like Jesus Christ. God became man so that we can know God and grow to become more like him, eventually transformed into his very likeness.

The same goes for our preaching and teaching: as a result of our communication, our listeners should be growing to think more like Jesus, to feel as Jesus felt, and to act as Jesus acted. In other words, life change.

TRY THESE TOOLS

PREACH APPLICATION

To preach or teach for life change means we must make application. No message is complete unless you drill down into how it applies to your listeners. Often this step gets tacked on at the end of a message or receives the least amount of our time and thought. If the purpose is life change, then we cannot allow the application to be an afterthought.

PREACH TO YOUR DIFFERENT AUDIENCES

Think through how exactly your message applies to different audiences. High school students may apply it in one way, parents in another, and seniors in still another way. (See pages 125–127.)

PREACH STEPS

When making the application, consider the steps you want your community to take to grow as disciples. (See pages 161–162). Of course, this presupposes you know what steps you want them to take.

Joshua, the great man of God, was given the privilege of leading the people of God into the Promised Land. To prepare them, he preached with specific application: leave your false Egyptian idols behind, and serve the living Lord. Basically he was preaching life change.

In our communication we want to inform in order to transform.

83

DON'T DEMAND; DON'T COMMAND

As Jesus passed on from there, he saw a man named Matthew sitting at the customs post. He said to him, "Follow me."

—Matthew 9:9

Father Michael: My mother always said, "Nobody is ever insulted to be invited." Who doesn't like to receive an invitation? When it arrives it is the most welcome kind of mail, whether the invitation is for a birthday party, an anniversary, a holiday, or a wedding. On the other hand, commands, when issued, rarely feel very good, even if they are reasonable or come urgently and with good reason from superiors. We'd much rather be asked. But better yet, we'd prefer to be invited.

That was Jesus' method. Over and over again, with Peter and Andrew, the woman at the well, the Gerasene demoniac, Zacchaeus, and of course, the tax collector, Matthew, he simply invited people to follow him.

So when did we in churchworld decide that the command mode was the way to go? Don't demand, don't command; invite people into your message.

84

CONNECT TO
THE ONE PERSON
YOU'RE TALKING TO

Now a man there named Zacchaeus, who was a
chief tax collector and also a wealthy man, was
seeking to see who Jesus was; but he could not
see him because of the crowd, for he was short
in stature. So he ran ahead and climbed a syca-
more tree in order to see Jesus, who was about
to pass that way. When he reached the place,
Jesus looked up and said to him, "Zacchaeus,
come down quickly, for today I must stay at
your house."

—Luke 19:2–5

When you are communicating to large groups, it is easy to struggle with
what to say. We know that every audience is coming from some perspective, one that might represent a very different perspective from the one
we've formed. Or perhaps there are divergent and conflicting views in the
crowd. Sometimes we can get overwhelmed by those facts, and we say
nothing of value so as not to offend anyone. Or we try to say everything to
please everyone.

There are basically three types of people listening to you. There are
those who are for you and with you, and there are those who are not, who
disagree with what you've got to say. The tendency for most of us, most of
the time, is to try to communicate to one of these two camps.

Meanwhile there is always a third group in any audience we speak to: the people in the middle who could go either way. Speak to them. You don't need to convince the convinced and you might not ever convert your critics, but you have a great shot at gaining a hearing and maybe winning the argument among the undecided.

Try to connect to the one man or woman in your audience you want to reach, and imagine you are having a conversation with him or her. Sometimes that can mean a person who isn't even real, an archetypal person. In *Rebuilt*, we described "Timonium Tim," the quintessential unchurched person we are trying to communicate with in our community. (Tim grew up Catholic but stopped going to church because it's boring and bad.) In reviewing messages, we will consistently ask, "What would Tim think of this message?"

Besides the crowds that he spoke to everywhere he went, there were some specific people Jesus wanted to reach. Zacchaeus was one of them, the guy Jesus came all the way to Jericho to talk to. Who is the one guy you're trying to reach?

85

MESSAGING IS A TEAM SPORT

And they all left him and fled.

—Mark 14:50

Velocity is speed. Mass is weight. In the project that is our parish, velocity is about getting people going further, faster, in the same discipleship direction. Mass is about getting more and more people doing it. When mass and velocity are combined, you have energy. That's what we want when it comes to our parish communication.

To make that happen in your parish, you need a team. Regardless of the size of your parish, and the size of your staff, a team of people is the key to effective communication.

Everyone, from the weekend preacher to the ushers and the after-Mass fellowship hosts, needs to be on the same page when it comes to what you are trying to communicate. That requires internal communication that precedes your general or church-wide communication. Probably everybody on your team is *with* your team and gets what you are trying to do (if not, you've got bigger issues than communication), but they need to hear your message, your mission, and your values over and over again. They (and you for that matter) can really never hear it enough.

> **Tom:** To that end, we are big proponents of meetings (okay, Michael is anyway), not for the sake of meetings but for the sake of sharing information. Before any kind of event, we will definitely have a meeting, and if it is a big one such as Christmas, we'll have a whole season

of meetings. In the course of an average weekend, our staff gathers for perhaps as many as four brief meetings; Saturday afternoon before the weekend cycle kicks in; Saturday evening, in view of how our first service went; Sunday morning first thing; and one final time on Sunday afternoon. The purpose of all these meetings is communication about what's going on with everyone who is helping make it happen.

We also have a weekly electronic newsletter for all staff and member ministers to bring them up to speed on what to expect when arriving on campus in the upcoming weekend. Likewise, we have a daily devotional for all parishioners, to keep the weekend message fresh in their minds and hopefully in their prayer.

The events of the Passion begin to descend into confusion and chaos as the disciples abandon Jesus and flee in fear. He knew it was coming; he understood that he would have to face the Cross alone. But that is not how he wants his Church to operate. Put time and effort into shaping your team into a cohesive whole through extensive and exacting internal communications.

86

NEVER GET
OVER THE PRIVILEGE

How beautiful upon the mountains are the feet
of the one bringing good news, announcing
peace, bearing good news, announcing salvation, saying to Zion, "Your God is King!"

—Isaiah 52:7

And how can people preach unless they are
sent? As it is written, "How beautiful are the feet
of those who bring [the] good news?"

—Romans 10:15

A good friend of ours works for a very prestigious public relations firm in
Washington, DC. Bob's firm represents high-powered professionals, glob-
ally influential organizations, and multinational corporations. One time,
he was gracious enough to arrange for a complimentary meeting with
members of his staff to help us with our website and social media strategy. When he introduced us to his team, he said, "Most of our clients are
searching for something to say. These guys actually have a message; they
just need to get a little better at packaging it."

Many companies simply look to make money (certainly a worthwhile
business objective). But they need to engage the service of public relations
professionals to help them find a worthwhile message in the pursuit of that
goal.

As the Church of Christ, we already have a message worth communicating. We don't have to find one.

Evangelion is the Greek word from which we get the English word "gospel," which means "good news." We are stewards of a message of incredibly good news that is, in fact, the greatest news of all, the greatest message ever. That should shine though all your preaching and teaching.

The book of the prophet Isaiah looks forward to a time when the Gospel will be preached and forecasts the incredible opportunity and privilege it will be. That time is our time, and that's our message. Never, never ever, get over the privilege.

87

STAY GREAT

When it had been reported to Sanballat, Tobi-
ah, Geshem the Arab, and our other enemies
that I had rebuilt the wall . . . Sanballat and
Geshem sent me this message: "Come, let us
hold council together at Chephirim in the plain
of Ono." They were planning to do me harm. I
sent messengers to them with this reply: "I am
engaged in a great enterprise and am unable to
come down."

—NEHEMIAH 6:1–3

Some time ago, we were in Chicago for discussions with our publisher related to this very book. Chicago is a great place, and we stayed at a hotel that was located in the "Loop," which is what Chicagoans call the commercial center of the city. We chose this particular hotel because of its proximity to our destination and also because we got a great deal on the rate. Never having heard of it, and not liking surprises, we toured the hotel's website.

Besides being a bargain, the place appeared to be quite elegant. Built on a monumental scale, in an optimum location, the hotel was the site of some great history and grand events, playing host to presidents and kings.

No kings around by the time we checked in.

Perhaps not intentionally or deliberately, but eventually this place had changed. The magnificent lobby got carved up into a crummy little corridor; the stylish dining room is now only a coffee shop (with really bad coffee); and the legendary bar is a shabby pool parlor. The once-lovely arcade of luxury boutiques has been reduced to junk shops. The guest rooms stopped getting decently updated and then stopped getting thoroughly cleaned some time ago. The splendor of the architecture and the integrity of the service had been compromised at every turn, reducing the majestic to the mundane. The place had an air of slow but steady death. Great became good, which became good enough, which drifted into not nearly good enough. How did that happen? When was the day that it became okay for one of the letters in the big rooftop sign to go dark and stay that way? How did the personnel policy change so that it was acceptable for staff members to choose not to greet guests with courtesy? Why was the decision ever made to allow the carpets to become filthy?

Who knows really? At some point in the life of this particular hotel, there was someone, or a whole critical mass of someones, who cared enough, probably passionately, to make sure their hotel was reaching a high bar of excellence. All remaining evidence suggests they were the best at what they did, way ahead of the pack. Then flash forward, and they're not.

Whatever happened at this hotel, the place tells a story. One day people stop noticing. Then they stop caring. Then they stop showing up. And then you've got a dump instead of a best-in-its-class destination. Suddenly what was working isn't anymore.

It can happen anywhere. It happens all the time in our parishes. It happens easiest of all in our preaching and teaching. It's just so effortless to give ourselves permission not to put in the effort, to cut corners, and to start settling for merely "good" and then "good enough." And then, long before you know it, your communication isn't that good at all. It isn't really working anymore. It no longer matters to you, and that will guarantee it matters not in the least to your congregation.

For innovators, creators, and lead agents in change of any kind, there is rarely a rulebook. They're just out there learning what great means in their field and doing great stuff better than anyone else.

Great communicators, like Nehemiah, understand the value of their message, and they stay on message despite distractions and even threats. Most important, they keep working at it. Your preaching and teaching matters and deserves your consistent and best efforts. Get great and then stay that way.

88

THE MESSAGE
IS ABOUT MOTIVATION

Do not be afraid, Mary, for you have found favor with God. Behold, you will conceive in your
womb and bear a son, and you shall name him
Jesus. He will be great and will be called Son of
the Most High, and the Lord God will give him
the throne of David his father, and he will rule
over the house of Jacob forever, and of his kingdom there will be no end.

—Luke 1:30–33

Often the changes we need to make in life are not rocket science. If you want to lose weight, burn more calories than you consume. If you want to get out of debt, cut down on your expenses. Changes in our spiritual life aren't usually complicated either. The spiritual habits of prayer, forgiveness, giving, and serving aren't difficult to understand, but often we struggle with them anyway. Why?

Quite simply, whether it's a diet, debt, or daily prayer, the status quo tends to rule our lives until we have a compelling or perhaps painful reason to change.

When it comes to evangelization and discipleship, we're talking about change and growth. But the old-fashioned approach, relying on guilt and fear, no longer works. Besides, that's not how Jesus taught us to do it anyway. Instead, we have to motivate people to change and inspire them to grow.

Remind people of the usefulness and utility of the Gospel, how well Christ's teaching actually works in our lives. Teach the blessings and rewards that the Bible promises in exchange for obedience.

Cast a vision for what God has in mind for those who follow and serve him. Focus people's attention on what their life will look like after they take that step. Show them the impact they will make on others. Share with them the larger story into which their lives can fit.

The first and greatest disciple of Jesus Christ was Mary. She steps into this role selflessly and quite courageously but not spontaneously. It happens in response to the invitation of the archangel Gabriel. His message was shocking for sure, but it was also profoundly motivational.

89

GOD IS THE MESSAGE

———————⌄———————

Grace and truth came through Jesus Christ.
—John 1:17

In our mission to make disciples of Jesus Christ in the age of the New Evangelization, we have to begin with the understanding that the people we're communicating to are steeped in distaste for or even hostility toward organized religion, skepticism of scripture, and a more or less outright rejection of the supernatural. And yet, study after study tells us the vast majority of people believe in God.

That's because we live in a culture that is essentially deistic. Deism has been around since the Enlightenment but has gained a lot of ground in our own time. It is basically the belief that creation and reason prove the existence of a God. But that's about it; that's all that's proved. Everything else is cast in doubt and up for debate. There is no revelation, and God has told us nothing about himself. He has created the world and set it to unfold according to natural laws. We are pretty much on our own. Many cultural and cradle Catholics could sum up their real beliefs in just this way. There are even people in our pews every single week who, more or less, are basically deists.

We have to begin and end there, with God.

Our communication should start with that fragile faith in a distant, detached God and begin to fill in the details. It is our job to let them know about a Father who planned for them from forever, formed them in their mothers' wombs, and gave them life and breath. We can introduce them to the Son who calls them to follow him and become more like him, serving the movement of his kingdom in our generation. Our communication must help people appreciate the mystery of the Spirit who walks with us daily and guides our steps when we cooperate in greater stewardship and service. Through our message, others can come to know the Spirit who changes lives, helps shape choices, and brings blessing both here and in eternity. The message we share is all about the grace of what God does for us and the truth of what he calls us to do.

To successfully rebuild your message you've got to be uncompromisingly clear about what that message is at its core. It is a message of grace and truth—these two together.

If all of your preaching and teaching were reduced to a single sermon, a final instruction, it wouldn't be about preaching or teaching anyway. It would be about witness. It's all about witness to grace and truth.

In other words, it's all about Jesus Christ—God's Holy Word.

REFERENCES
AND RESOURCES

The following have all been influential in the formation of the concepts and ideas found in this book.

BOOKS AND DOCUMENTS

Collins, Jim. *Good to Great*. New York: HarperCollins, 2001.

———. *How the Mighty Fall*. New York: HarperCollins, 2009.

Collins, Jim, and Jerry Porras. *Built to Last*. New York: Harper Business, 2002.

Dulles, Avery. *The Resilient Church: The Necessity and Limits of Adaptation*. Garden City, NY: Doubleday, 1977.

Ferguson, Dave, Jon Ferguson, and Eric Bramlet. *The Big Idea: Focus the Message, Multiply the Impact*. Grand Rapids, MI: Zondervan, 2007.

Francis. *The Joy of the Gospel*. Washington, DC: The United States Catholic Conference of Bishops, 2013.

Gladwell, Malcolm. *The Tipping Point: How Little Things Can Make a Big Difference*. Boston: Little, Brown, 2000.

Godin, Seth. *Tribes: We Need You to Lead Us*. New York: Portfolio, 2008.

Groechel, Craig. *It: How Churches and Leaders Can Get It and Keep It*. Grand Rapids, MI: Zondervan, 2008.

Heath, Chip, and Dan Heath. *Made to Stick*. New York: Random House, 2008.

———. *Switch: How to Change Things When Change Is Hard*. New York: Broadway Books, 2010.

Humes, James C. *Speak Like Churchill, Stand Like Lincoln*. New York: Crown Publishing Group, 2002.

Hybels, Bill. *Axiom: Powerful Leadership Proverbs*. Grand Rapids, MI: Zondervan, 2008.

———. *The Volunteer Revolution*. Grand Rapids, MI: Zondervan, 2004.

John Paul II. *Christifideles Laici*. Vatican: The Holy See, 1998.

———. *Dies Domini*. Vatican: The Holy See, 1998.

Kinnaman, David, and Gabe Lyons. *Unchristian: What a New Generation Really Thinks About Christianity . . . and Why it Matters*. Grand Rapids, MI: Baker Books, 2008.

Lencioni, Patrick. *The Advantage*. San Francisco: Jossey-Bass, 2012.

———. *The Five Dysfunctions of a Team.* San Francisco: Jossey-Bass, 2002.

Lyons, Gabe. *The Next Christians.* New York: Doubleday, 2010.

Mallon, James. *Divine Renovation.* Toronto: Novalis, 2014.

Mancini, Will. *Church Unique.* San Francisco: Jossey-Bass, 2008.

Rainer, Thom. *Breakout Churches.* Grand Rapids, MI: Zondervan, 2005.

Rainer, Thom, and Eric Geiger. *Simple Church.* Nashville: Broadman and Holman, 2006.

Ratzinger, Joseph. *The Spirit of the Liturgy.* San Francisco: Ignatius Press, 2000.

Second Vatican Council. *Lumen Gentium.* Vatican: The Holy See, 1964.

———. *Sacrosanctum Concilium.* Vatican: The Holy See, 1963.

Stanley, Andy. *Deep & Wide.* Grand Rapids, MI: Zondervan, 2012.

Stanley, Andy, and Lane Jones. *Communicating for a Change: Seven Keys to Irresistible Communication.* Colorado Springs: Multnomah Books, 2006.

Stanley, Andy, Reggie Joiner, and Lane Jones. *7 Practices of Effective Ministry.* Colorado Springs: Multnomah Books, 2004.

Stevens, Tim, and Tony Morgan. *Simply Strategic Stuff.* Loveland, CO: Group Publishing, 2004.

Warren, Rick. *The Purpose Driven Church.* Grand Rapids, MI: Zondervan, 1995.

WEBSITES AND ONLINE RESOURCES

Elevation Church in Matthews, NC. elevationchurch.org.

Lifechurch.TV in Edmund, OK. open.lifechurch.tv.

Morgan, Tony. *Tony Morgan Live* (blog). tonymorganlive.com.

NewSpring Church in Anderson, SC. newspring.cc.

Northpoint Church in Alpharetta, GA. northpoint.org. Resources from Northpoint Church can be purchased at store.northpoint.org.

Preaching Rocket. The Rocket Company: Cumming, GA. therocketcompany.com.

Rainer, Thom S. *Thom S. Rainer* (blog). thomrainer.com.

Saddleback Church in Lake Forest, CA. saddleback.com. Resources from Saddleback Church can be purchased at www.saddlebackresources.com.

CHURCH OF THE NATIVITY RESOURCES

Church of the Nativity in Timonium, MD. churchnativity.tv. On Facebook at facebook.com/churchnativity.

Rebuilt Parish. rebuiltparish.com. *Rebuilt* podcast at https://itunes.apple.com/us/podcast/rebuilt-podcast/id645574414?mt=2.

Wesley, Christopher. *Marathon Youth Ministry* (blog). christopherwesley.org.

White, Michael. *Make Church Matter* (blog). nativitypastor.tv. On Twitter @nativitypastor.

Tom Corcoran received his bachelor's degree from Loyola University Maryland and studied theology at Franciscan University of Steubenville. Corcoran has served Church of the Nativity in a variety of roles that give him a unique perspective on parish ministry and leadership. First hired as a youth minister, Corcoran has also served as coordinator of children's ministry and director of small groups.

Corcoran is associate to the pastor and is responsible for weekend message development, strategic planning, and staff development. He is the coauthor of *Rebuilt*—which narrates the story of Nativity's rebirth—and *Tools for Rebuilding*. When he is not working, Corcoran enjoys spending time with his wife, Mia, and their seven children, who are homeschooled in Parkville, Maryland.

Michael White earned his bachelor's degree from Loyola University Maryland and his graduate degrees in sacred theology and ecclesiology from the Pontifical Gregorian University in Rome. After being ordained a priest of the Archdiocese of Baltimore, he worked for five years as personal secretary to Cardinal William Keeler, who was then archbishop. During that time, White served as the director of the papal visit of Pope John Paul II to Baltimore.

During White's tenure as pastor at Church of the Nativity, the church has almost tripled in weekend attendance from 1,400 to more than 4,000. More importantly, commitment to the mission of the Church has grown, evidenced by the significant increase of giving and service in ministry, and much evidence of genuine spiritual renewal. White is the coauthor of *Rebuilt*—which narrates the story of Nativity's rebirth—and *Tools for Rebuilding*. The books have sold more than 100,000 copies combined.